Praise for

FORGIVENESS

"An unforgettable story about the power of forgiveness, set against one of the darkest periods in Canada's history. Mark Sakamoto tells his family's story with grace and at times brutal honesty. Painful and poignant, Forgiveness is a testament to the resilience of the human spirit." —Mellissa Fung, author of Under an Afghan Sky

"A relatable journey of real-life ups and downs—humble reminders, throughout, to be more kind and forgiving of others and to ourselves, that letting go is to be grateful for life's challenges as tests of courage and willingness to forge through fear and disappointment. This book shares many examples of powerful life lessons that inspire us to embrace change as a gift from learning, and [remind us] that making peace with our past is possible if we hold on to what we've learned from our experiences and let go of what we cannot change."
—Shania Twain

"Mark Sakamoto's family story shows how individuals—the author's Canadian grandfather, a POW of the Japanese, and his Japanese-Canadian grandmother, sent to a work camp in Alberta—ultimately make their own history. This is a quintessential Canadian story, where family history is not forgotten but does not imprison its participants." —Nathan M. Greenfield, author of The Damned

"This is an astonishing book, part memoir, part saga of two Canadian families, Japanese and Canadian, that were at war with each other and found peace and forgiveness together. It is a funny, heartbreaking story of a family scarred by history's pain and their own self-destructiveness, yet redeemed by stoic endurance and the capacity for forgiveness. You're going to remember this book."
—Michael Ignatieff

FORGIVENESS

A Gift from My Grandparents

Mark Sakamoto

HARPER
PERENNIAL

Published by Harper Perennial, an imprint of HarperCollins Publishers Ltd

First published by HarperCollins Publishers Ltd in a hardcover edition: 2014
This Harper Perennial trade paperback edition: 2015

HarperCollins books may be purchased for educational, business,
or sales promotional use through our Special Markets Department.

HarperCollins Publishers Ltd
2 Bloor Street East, 20th Floor
Toronto, Ontario, Canada
M4W 1A8

www.harpercollins.ca

Library and Archives Canada Cataloguing in Publication
information is available upon request

ISBN 9781443417983

Printed and bound in the United States of America
RRD 9 8 7 6 5 4 3 2 1

All photographs courtesy of the author with the exception of those on pages 86 and 114
(Public Archives of Canada), and 131 (Library and Archives Canada/PA–187673).

For my daughters, Miya and Tomi,
so you know what you are made of

CONTENTS

Prologue

PART 1: ENTRY ISLAND
1 Castaways / 11
2 Cast Away / 39
3 No Good / 57

PART 2: THE WAR YEARS
4 Pearl Harbor / 69
5 Celtic, British Columbia / 85
6 Ralph's War / 103
7 Mitsue's War / 133

PART 3: RELEASE
8 Going Home / 153
9 Mark 11:25 / 163
10 Amen / 171

PART 4: THE GIFT
11 The Gas City / 177
12 Breakup / 193
13 Breakdown / 203
14 The Boys Are on Their Way / 223
15 Journey's End / 235

Epilogue / 241
Acknowledgments / 243
Photo Captions / 247

Prologue

I held the cassette gently in my hands, flipping it from side to side. It felt like a relic. I know that in actuality an audio cassette is simply a spool of magnetically coated tape, wound through two spools encased in a protective plastic shell. But the transparent rectangle in the middle of the cassette was a window into my past. My mom was in there. She was laughing in there, she was carefree, she was in love. The cassette was thirty-two years, four months and sixteen days old. My mom was alive in there. She was alive and well.

I'm ashamed to admit that I had had the tape in my possession for over a year. I had held it in my hands countless times. I would round the edge with my fingers, staring at it, dwelling on it. This outdated piece of technology made my mind race and my heart ache. I cursed each time that cold wave came over me. I knew the routine. There was that one memory—different every time—that triggered loss of breath and then heaving and tears. There was the thought that I should regain control of myself. There was the failure of that thought. There were more tears as I surrendered.

I was eight all over again.

I've never had the strength to play the tape. Sometimes I wish it had never come into my possession. Thirteen months earlier, my grandpa Sakamoto died. Hideo Sakamoto was ninety-six and the local newspaper ran a story about him. Harold Brucker, an old customer of his, recalled him running up and down the grocery store stairs with one-hundred-pound potato sacks.

"He was like the Atlas Man," Harold reportedly said to the *Medicine Hat News*.

As an adult Hideo weighed only 124 pounds, but he was simply indefatigable. Those burlap potato sacks would cut into his bony shoulders. The weight of his family, too, rested on those sore shoulders.

Sometimes he was wrong, like in 1954, when he decided to plant all the crops two weeks early only to have them completely wiped out in a flash frost. But he was right when it mattered. His life's most important decision was a grand-slam home run. He married an angel. Mitsue Margaret Sakamoto was his wife for sixty-eight years.

Throughout his married life, as he went about his day, he would repeat her name over and over again under his breath. Just the idea of her seemed to keep him going. "Mits . . . Mits . . . Mits . . ." he would whisper.

He was meditating on her. She was his *koan*. She was his everything. I'm sure I'll live my whole life and never witness a love so necessary.

Two days after Grandpa's funeral, I went over to my grandma Sakamoto's. Parking in the driveway, I could see her through the kitchen window, standing at the sink looking down, hard at work, no doubt on some dish for me to eat.

She has spent tens of thousands of hours in that very spot, thinly slicing beef for *sukiyaki*, mashing *kamaboko*, thawing *tako*, mixing the filling for *gyoza*, draining *ohitashi*, rolling *maki sushi*. She moves through the kitchen with an ancient grace. I have spent my whole life watching her cook.

But it always started with tea. Piping hot, *matcha* green tea.

As I walked through the side door that day, my grandma was drying her hands with a dishcloth. This scene, too, had played out a million times.

"Hi, Gram," I said as I took off my shoes.

"Hi, come in, come in. I'm making rice."

We met in the middle of the kitchen and hugged. I kissed her cheek. Her face was round and elegant. Her skin at eighty-nine was still soft and vibrant. There were many years when she went without, but her appearance did not betray that hardship. She could pass for sixty-five. At five-foot-seven she was taller than most Japanese women. She was reserved and exceptionally polite. But this gentle exterior masked a fierceness and pride that has served as the foundation for every single person in her family. And *her* family it is. She is our candle. Our entire family delighted in sharing her with as many people as we could. Countless friends had paraded through the same side door I had just entered.

Grandma opened the cupboard and pulled out two small Japanese *ocha* cups. I caught a glimpse of my grandpa's cup sitting where it always has, on the bottom shelf, first cup on the left. We sat down. The kitchen table was littered with sympathy cards, way more than you'd expect for a ninety-six-year-old man. The broken handwriting of the card just to my right was unmistakable. It was from my maternal grandfather, who lived just down the Trans-Canada Highway in Calgary.

A life well lived. With love & sympathy, Ralph MacLean.

I smiled and turned back to my grandma.

"How are you feeling? Did you sleep well?" I asked.

"Oh, I'm okay. You know, I miss him. It's so quiet here now. But I couldn't die before him."

It's true. He would have been completely lost.

The tea had finished steeping. I poured her a cup, then one for myself. She nodded a thank you and ran her index finger across the ceramic lip. She was lost momentarily in thought or grief, I couldn't tell for sure, but then she snapped to attention.

"Want some fish? Or *tsukemono*?" She giggled.

She knew I loved *tsukemono*. She knew everyone's favourite dish and always had it at the ready—it was her welcome mat.

"Sure, Gram—thanks." I smiled, knowing the chain reaction I had just initiated.

Tsukemono: in the fridge, in a ceramic bowl wrapped in Saran, second shelf to the left. Two small plates: cupboard to right of the sink where the cups are, bottom shelf. Chopsticks: same cupboard, top shelf, in the middle between the rice bowls and the teacups. *Shoyu*: cupboard to the left of the sink, top shelf, beside the blue bowl of white sugar with the ornamental spoon from Niagara Falls.

This kitchen is the one place in the world where I could function completely blind. Everything is in the exact place it has been for my entire thirty-four years. In my mind's eye it always seems so much larger than it actually is. The kitchen is essentially a galley. The counter runs across the north wall, with the stove and fridge side by side and the kitchen table hovering on the other side of them. The south wall is covered with bamboo wallpaper sent by my grandpa's cousin in Tokyo. The table and chairs are standard 1960s fare. It's actually retro-kitschy. It is also the most comforting place in my universe.

When I was in grade school, I would feign illness to spend the day at my grandparents'. My elementary school was just down the road from their house, a six-minute drive if you didn't hit the one red light at the bottom of the hill. Peering through the school's main foyer doors, I'd wait to see my grandpa's lime green 1979 GM pickup crest the hill. On the way home, we'd stop at the video store and Grandpa would bellow a heavily accented "Hell-ooo," which actually sounded more like "Herr-ooo," to no one in particular and flash his toothy grin as we walked in. Man, that guy could smile.

By the time we got home, the salty sea smell of *miso* soup would be filling the kitchen and the futon would be laid out on the living room floor by the television. Grandma would greet me at the door; she'd feel my forehead and look at my face.

"You're warm," she'd say, lying.

We were conspiring to spend the day together. I loved being in on it. Our collusion went unspoken.

I'd spend the time slurping tofu chunks and *miso* soup, drinking ginger ale and watching ninja movies with Grandpa.

"So, what are your plans today, Gram?" I asked, coming out of my reverie.

"Ahh, I have work to do. He kept so much junk."

This was a monumental understatement. Hideo Sakamoto had been a pack rat in the first degree, a borderline hoarder. Their garage was crammed to the ceiling with old farm supplies, thousands of yards of twine, hundreds of dirty old baskets, twenty-eight shovels, boots for a small army. There were thirty-one sets of work gloves, all size small. I could see his crooked fingers slipping into them for another day of hard work that would only make his arthritis worse. Their garage was a dusty monument to toil under the Alberta prairie sky.

The basement was no better. It was filled with remnants of a long life spent far from friends and family. There were boxes upon boxes of letters from Japan stacked to the ceiling, and unpacked *omiyage*, gifts from visiting relatives. There were farm invoices and bank statements that proved you really could live on love. Grandma had started to tackle those first.

"I found a few boxes for you." She was almost whispering as the tea steam rose from the cup on the table in front of her. "Do you want to see them?"

I nodded. It was a lie.

We made our way down the stairs. She descended slowly but deliberately. I followed her into the rectangular rumpus room, half living room, half storage container. There were two old couches against opposing walls with a futon between them. When my brother Daniel and I were little, we'd strip down to our white Fruit of the Looms, give ourselves gonchy-pulls, and engage in the ancient art of sumo wrestling—or at least our version of it. Fortunately we grew out of that. In aggregate, I have probably spent more waking hours of my life in this room than in any other. Daniel and I arrested thousands of villains, vanquished countless storm troopers, and generally kept the world safe in this single twelve-by-thirty-foot room.

There were two boxes in front of the futon. Grandma kneeled to open the first one.

"This stuff is all from Fiji," she explained.

When my dad graduated from college, the first job he took was at a hotel in Suva, Fiji. It was a fifteen-room facility located on the south side of the island. The owner was a Canadian who had made his money in the lumber industry and struck out to find his own heaven. He hit pay dirt. My dad thought so too. Stanley Gene Sakamoto would start each day eating pineapples and mangos and then wade into the Pacific Ocean for his morning swim. He was twenty-four years old and living in paradise (aside from a few inconvenient political coups).

Three months later, my mom followed him. They quickly made friends with other expats and locals. My mom got a job at a childcare centre. She would marvel at how happy life could be in the midst of relative poverty. Laughter was as abundant as sunshine. She would watch the children climb the coconut trees in their bare feet for hours. For her, it was a religious experience. There, perhaps for the first time in her life, she felt close to God.

"Oh, this should go back to your grandpa MacLean," Grandma said as she passed me a green velvet case embossed in gold with the Queen's face. It was the Pacific Star medal.

"He must have given it to my mom before she left for Fiji," I said.

I knew this to be one of the many medals my grandpa MacLean had received during the war. My mom had shown it to me before. It hung on coloured ribbons: red, narrow dark blue, green, narrow yellow, green, narrow light blue, and red. The colours represented the forests and beaches of Hong Kong. The medal had been awarded in recognition of service in the Honk Kong theatre of war. It was set in blood red velvet. My grandpa MacLean was, in every sense of the word, a war hero, though he'd never call himself that. He had only done what needed to be done. He tried to kill—and tried his best to avoid being killed by—people who looked like the woman who was now carefully passing me his medal. The people trying to kill my grandpa all those years ago looked like his first-born grandson. They looked like me.

When Grandpa MacLean talks about the war, which is more often as he gets on in years, he always says he spent it trying to keep his head down and his buddies alive. Some made it, some did not. When he lost his strength to fight on, he prayed. Someone heard him. He beat astronomical odds to do it, but he survived.

My grandma Sakamoto and my grandpa MacLean shared a deep and unrelenting respect and love for each other. As impossible as it may seem, Mitsue Margaret Sakamoto and Ralph Augustus MacLean saw themselves in one another.

"Okay, I'll make sure Grandpa gets it back," I said.

Satisfied, my grandma nodded.

Her hands darted back into the box and emerged with a hand-drawn picture of the hut in which my parents had lived, a beautiful thatch peaked structure with rows of palm trees on either side. Instinctively, I smelled the picture, but no ocean fragrance remained. The hut was right on the beach and I could picture my mom and dad strolling hand in hand as they watched the sun dive into the ocean, leaving the day a parting gift of streaks of pink and orange. I placed the picture carefully on the futon as Grandma continued the excavation. An album of pictures, mostly of friends dining on white fish and drinking Fiji Bitter beer.

"Life looked pretty good," I said.

My grandma giggled. "Oh, and Dar dropped this off too," she said.

And there it was: the cassette. I knew exactly what it was as soon as I saw it. She handed it to me as I put on a brave face.

"Her voice . . . it's been so long."

My mom and Darlene, her favourite cousin and best friend, would mail cassette tapes back and forth while my mom was in Fiji. She was pregnant with me and Dar had just had her first son, Eric.

A new life was beginning for both of them, and they were sharing this newness together, across the vast Pacific Ocean.

My grandma had moved on to the second box and I realized that I hadn't heard a word she said for the past five minutes. I sensed that heaving feeling approach like an unwelcome acquaintance.

"Grandma," I said, "I have a few errands to run. I'll come back and help you later this aft, okay?"

"Of course," she said.

She was feeling my forehead all over again.

PART 1

Entry Island

CHAPTER 1

Castaways

It started out innocently enough. I should not have been caught unawares. Grandpa Ralph does have a habit of travelling with one family member at a time. I can't quite pin down when that began. Cousin Christine went with him to Hawaii. Uncle Blake accompanied him to China. He wants to show his family the world. When my turn came, I was just wrapping up my first year of law school in Halifax. He rang me up. He knew I had not spoken to my mom in months. Neither had he.

"Thinking about going home. Thought maybe I might swing by Halifax and take you with me."

This was a trip of a lifetime. His lifetime. It would almost certainly be the last time he returned home. He made no bones about that.

"Well, I'm eighty-three now. How many times can I make the trek back there, eh?"

My grandpa never let sentiment run his show. He didn't quite need a cane yet, but he had purchased one. It was still in the box, in the spare bedroom off the kitchen, where he did his ironing. It was waiting. He knew its time was coming.

"So, whatdya say?"

There was no hesitation on my end of the line. I was up for this road trip.

"I'm in, Grandpa! I can't wait."

All I really knew about the Magdalen Islands was their shape. Grandpa had an old framed map on his basement wall that I had studied several times. The islands were a tiny little sliver, sitting all alone in the vast Gulf of the St. Lawrence. They looked like an amoeba under a microscope.

Three weeks later, en route to pick up Grandpa at the Halifax International Airport, I had to pull over twice as horizontal rain, coming in sideways off the ocean, blinded my view of the highway.

I spotted him standing outside the airport terminal pickup area, suitcase at his feet. He was, of course, braving the elements. He waved when he saw my blue Volkswagen. He knew it well. I'd driven him around in it when I lived with him in Calgary while I went to university. He picked up his suitcase and walked over to the curb, his bowlegged gait seemingly as strong as ever. I was glad to see that he had left his cane in the closet. I pulled over and before I could get out to give him a hand, he hopped in.

"Some rain, eh?" he said.

"Just another day on the east coast. Scared of a little rain?" I said, teasing.

"Oh, I'm no pantywaist—I'll manage."

We laughed, but I didn't mention the two stops I had made en route to the airport. We got caught up as we drove into the city. Grandpa made a point to keep in touch with family, but he has never been one to dither on the phone. He'll call you up and talk for a few minutes: the weather, school, his bum knee; then, abruptly, he'll say, "Well, I won't keep you. Talk to you later," and the line goes dead. It is a cordial hit-and-run.

So there was quite a bit to go over. We reviewed how all the family members were doing. He had hired a new cleaning lady because the previous one had moved to Regina. He had fixed a piece of carpet that had lifted on the stairs.

"Darn near tripped on it twice."

We were just entering city limits when he let me know that, just by coincidence, his niece Marian and her husband, Hans, would be out on the island at the same time as us. This was a great little surprise to me. Just after Marian was born, her father died of lung disease and her mother, my grandpa's sister Ada, asked him to be Marian's godfather. He stepped into her life in a way that has left an endearing mark. It is impossible for her to speak of my grandpa without tearing up a little.

Marian was born with an underdeveloped leg and an overdeveloped heart. She has a left shoe with a thickened sole and she walks with a bit of a shuffle. She always required a little extra attention, and she got it from my grandpa. Marian lives for her family and she has never forgotten the extra time, the extra love Ralph Augustus MacLean gave to her.

Marian married a German man named Hans whom she met in Calgary in the 1940s. Hans is a no-nonsense man armed with a quick wit. My mom loved him—he could take a ribbing and dish one out. I imagine a lot of back and forth between the two of them. When my dad started coming around, Hans took Mom aside and cautioned her. He liked my dad well enough—a lot, actually—but he felt it incumbent on him to ensure my mom took a cold hard look at the situation.

"You need to think about how your children would fare out there in the real world. We know just how cruel it can be."

I'm not sure whether my mom took Hans's advice to heart, but I know she received it warmly. He was looking out for his niece, just as my grandpa had looked out for Hans's wife so many years before.

When we got to my apartment, Jade had a hearty meal on the stove already. Grandpa is always ready for food. It really doesn't matter what time, day or night. Jade knows how he loves his sweets: a cake was baking in the oven. He smiled as we came through the apartment door.

Our place was so small that we had to eat in the living room. Grandpa didn't mind. He was happy to be back in Halifax, and he has always had such affection for Jade. We spent the night chatting about the few months he had lived in the city, only a few blocks from our apartment on Ogilvy Street, just off tree-lined South Street with its old-world mansions. We didn't have the money to live there—and Grandpa certainly didn't when he lived here either.

Grandpa slept in our bed. Jade and I folded out our IKEA futon couch and slept in the living room.

The next day, Grandpa and I drove across the Confederation Bridge and boarded a ferry to Grindstone, Magdalen Islands, six hours away on the open sea. The Gulf of St. Lawrence with its vast horizon and the salty sea breeze felt thoroughly oceanic.

The captain alerted his passengers that we would dock in thirty minutes. I grabbed the ice-cold railing on the ship's deck and squinted to see our destination.

Grandpa looked at me with a wry smile. "Toto, I've a feeling we're not in Kansas anymore," he said.

The landscape came into focus. The island looked like it had been bottled up into a time capsule in the 1800s. Houses speckled the hillside willy-nilly. Whoever had planned the island had clearly had no training. As we entered the harbour we passed Entry Island. A couple of miles long, it still had a one-room schoolhouse and six small farmhouses that looked like they had been built for the set of *Little House on the Prairie*.

My grandpa pondered as we passed.

"You know, I've never set foot on that island. I really should. I came to know so many of the boys who grew up there."

He had good reason to visit. Turns out, we all do. On a per capita basis, few places have given more blood and treasure to ensure our way of life than Entry Island; this little protruding speck of rock in the harbour of a slightly larger protruding speck of rock provided more volunteers to the Second World War than almost any other place in the Dominion. The whole island deserves a medal.

Almost every man on the island went to war. Entire families were killed. The Arsenault boys signed up. The Chanell brothers, all five of them, went. Few came back.

"They were all fine, fine men. They could shoot and they sure knew how to hang together. Guess they had been doing that all their lives on that plot of land," Grandpa said.

I spotted a large church that seemed too big for the island. I pointed it out.

"It's the Memorial. Entry Island folks erected it soon after the war. It's as close to a Royal Rifles Memorial as we're going to get," Grandpa explained.

He was thinking of those boys, wondering what their lives would have been like had they lived to his age. It was making his eyes well up, making him bite his stiff Scottish lip.

We docked, and as I drove off the boat, I felt further away from my life than I ever had. We were headed directly to Grandpa's old home. He didn't even want to drop off our bags where we would be staying first.

"Let's just get there," he said.

It was his duty to pay his respects to his old home. I knew he had mixed emotions about it. He loved this place. He hated this place. He was drawn to it and yet he wanted to flee as soon as he could.

The house itself sat on a corner edged by a jagged cliff. Pleasant Bay was visible in the distance. The two-storey house had not changed much since Grandpa left. It clung to the land, looking angry and leaning into the wind. I felt like I was visiting a tombstone.

He walked around the outside of the house like he would a museum. He was attached to it, but he kept his distance. He was no longer of this place; it did not hold him as it once had. He was free from it, but he still carried its weight on his shoulders.

We walked out past the potato patch—now completely overgrown—to the cliffs. It was a steep dive down. As a child, Grandpa would have been scolded—or worse—had he ventured this close to the edge. Now he paused four feet from it. His brown leather oxford shoes inched forward another two feet. I wondered if this was a childhood habit, or if he was worried about his bum knee.

"I'd imagine a different life from this spot," he said.

This view of sea and sky—emptiness—was his only window to the world. He could shape it however he wanted. A gust of sea wind blew hard against our faces. My windbreaker flapped like a naval flag. Grandpa took one step back, but quickly brought his foot right back into place. He was still a stubborn old fighter—he wouldn't be pushed around by some damn wind.

"Exactly the same as it was sixty years ago. I can just close my eyes and be back . . ."

We turned to make our way back to the car. I saw Grandpa pull out one of the white linen hankies he keeps in the back pocket of his trousers and quickly wipe his eye. Maybe it was the wind. We walked down the gravel laneway without saying a word.

I opened the passenger door and Grandpa slowly lowered himself in, holding the windshield as a brace. He let out a grunt when he was in the seat, followed, as always, by a cheerful "Okay—I'm good—thanks." I closed the door as he did up his seat belt, then walked around the back and got in the driver's seat.

We were in a bit of a hurry. We were headed to Grosse Île, which was tucked away in the northeast corner of the island. Grandpa always stayed with his cousin Margaret when he came home, which was about every ten years. Margaret was sure to have dinner ready by now.

Margaret's house was straight out of a children's tale. Like her, the house was tiny, old, and full of warmth. Everything was small and made out of wood. Every tabletop was fitted with a knitted doily. You never knew when a teapot might show up. There was a painted cuckoo clock above the archway that led from the living room into the dining area and kitchen. Neither Margaret nor her house quite fit in the twenty-first century.

Margaret embraced us and poured us tea. Halfway through the first cup, a truck came barrelling up her gravel driveway. Through the window we saw the rusted-out Chevy swerve as the driver tried to light a cigarette. It looked like his eyes were closed. He was drunk. "Right pissed" were Margaret's words. We smelled whisky before we heard the door open.

Margaret met her brother Frederick in the foyer.

"You can't come in here now. You go home, make a pot of coffee, and come back when you're presentable," she told him.

Grandpa explained to me that Frederick had been thrown out of Margaret's house more times than he'd been thrown out of the local tavern. He put up no fight.

"I'll see ya soon, Ralph!" he yelled as the door closed. A few minutes later the engine rattled away.

Margaret apologized profusely. It was unnecessary, of course, but she was mightily embarrassed. We sat down to a wonderful dinner of herring, lobster, and mashed potatoes. We drank milk. Margaret spent the dinner updating Grandpa on who had left and who had died.

Frederick dutifully returned four-and-a-half hours later smelling of coffee and cigarettes. It seemed as though he had willed himself sober so he could see my grandpa. His mission was simple: he wanted us to come to his house so he could give us his stash of canned haddock.

Grandpa could not say no to this gift; it would be a devastating insult. Fortunately, there was a lobster trap in the cab of Frederick's truck, giving us an excuse to follow him to his place in our rental car. We passed the post office, the graveyard, and two rabbits. The dark and the fog conspired against me as I struggled to follow Frederick's rear lights. There was not a street light to be seen.

We wound our way through a wooded area as the road deteriorated into a well-worn trail. Houses appeared out of the woods like ghosts. We pulled into a muddy ditch that served as a driveway, climbed out, and carefully made our way up to a rickety veranda.

The house was a dump. It reeked of whisky, canning brine, and sweat. It had not seen a cleaning product in a decade. The coffeepot had been left on. There was a canister of coffee whitener and an overflowing ashtray on the small kitchen table.

Frederick invited us to sit. The three kitchen chairs look liable to buckle. We took our chances and sat as he rifled through the cabinet under the sink for his stash—our gift. Half of Frederick's body was under his sink; it was as if he were rooting under the deck of a boat. He emerged with a sly grin, exposing broken, nicotine-stained teeth.

"Here you be," he said, holding out four Mason jars jammed full of haddock. Grandpa was clearly eager to leave and after some small talk about recent fish hauls and mutual friends, he used his time-tested escape hatch: "Well, we won't keep you."

"Don't want to stay for a nightcap?"

"Oh no, we've had a long day of travel."

And with that, we were off.

We were both glad to return to Margaret's. Her house hugged us as we came in. Grandpa took the spare room upstairs, I took the living-room couch. There was a small TV on top of a three-drawer cabinet. I turned it on and surfed the few channels Margaret was able to receive. The TV was placed in such a manner that you could really only see it if you were lying on the couch as I was. There was dust on the "on" knob. Watching CNN in Margaret's living room, I felt strangely out of place.

I woke to the sound of frying eggs and the smell of coffee. I could hear the shower going. I stretched and untangled myself from the three blankets I had slept under. The top one was an old Hudson's Bay blanket; I could almost see the paper catalogue it would have been ordered from, the one that came in the mail from the mainland.

In the kitchen, a CorningWare coffee percolator was brewing on the stovetop. The cast-iron frying pan had clearly cooked thousands upon thousands of eggs. I sat at the small kitchen table just behind the cupboard that separated the kitchen and the dining room. Margaret spun around with an enormous smile.

"Good morning, dear. I hope that you were comfortable enough on that old couch. Oh, how I wish I had another bed for you to have a proper sleep in."

I could tell she had been up half the night worrying about the sleeping arrangements.

"I had a great sleep. I hope the TV didn't bother you," I reassured her.

"Not at all, dear. I'm glad someone got some use out of it."

While I poured my coffee, Margaret dished me a heaping plate: four eggs, salted fish, two pieces of homemade bread, all smothered with fresh butter. Grandpa came in and sat down beside me with a smile.

After breakfast, he and I struck out for a drive around his old stomping grounds. We were hardly out of Margaret's front door before we stumbled into his memories. Almost everything was exactly as it had been when he was a child. We stopped the car at a valley and walked over the first hill to find his school. Behind the school was a clearing, more of a mossy bog that would ice over come winter. It was the local hockey rink.

"Seems like I spent my whole childhood in that clearing," he said.

He told me there were two teams. The Uproaders lived up the road from the school and the Downroaders lived below it. Grandpa was an Uproader along with his brother Ford, his cousin Walter MacLean, Harold Patton, Deighton Aitken, brothers David and Robert Grey, and Michael Sumarah. The Downroaders donned Toronto Maple Leafs jerseys, while the Uproaders sported the jerseys of the Chicago Blackhawks. Michael Sumarah's father, a Syrian immigrant who owned the dry goods store, had purchased the jerseys from the Hudson's Bay catalogue—the same one from which Margaret would have selected her blanket.

Fellow Uproader Deighton Aitken was Grandpa's closest chum and his right-winger. Deighton loved to say the word *Judas*. He'd scream against the frigid air: "Judas—pass me the puck, Ralphie!" Deighton always wanted the puck. He was always on the make for the next goal.

After the first period Mrs. Grey, Robert's mother, would usually come out with hot chocolate for all the boys. Hot chocolate under the stars with the game underway made for some of the finest nights

in Grandpa MacLean's memory. Although it was a warm breezy summer day, I could hear the blades carve into the ice and see the vapour rising from his mouth.

We lingered around the marshy rink for a while. Grandpa wanted to imagine being on the ice for one last skate as an Uproader, but we ran the risk of our shoes sinking in the mud. As we climbed back up the hill, Grandpa took a last look. He didn't say anything, but I know he saw twelve kids wearing Leafs and Blackhawks jerseys, some leaning on their sticks, some skating. He heard an echo of *Judas* off the pine trees.

We pressed on down the winding road and came to the local coffee shop. It was a tired-looking, smoke-stained place with six tables and some old bar-room chairs. I felt like we had stepped into an ATCO trailer. But the people huddled inside were some of the warmest I had ever met. It was the kind of place where, as the door opened, everyone paused to see who was joining them. They smiled with anticipation.

Today, they looked us over and I could tell everyone had the same question in their minds: Who are his people? I was a write-off on that front—I was clearly a "come from away." But they got forensic with Grandpa. Eyes were squinting, searching for a telltale family feature: Big ears? A particular nose?

I was looking through the room for a table to sit at and quickly get out of everyone's line of sight when I noticed that Grandpa was scanning their faces too, on the hunt for familiarity. From a table near the back of the room just beside the men's washroom came a holler. "MacLean!" It rang out with the excitement of a call of "Bingo!" Grandpa had been identified. Three old ladies at the table closest to us nodded in agreement. We had apparently been tagged and fit for release. We meandered our way to the back table and shook hands with one of Grandpa's old acquaintances. He was a member of the Sumarah clan—a cousin, I think. The family still owned the general store, and the man told us they had dramatically increased their operations by moving into the business of smoking fish.

These folks were tough. They stubbornly clung to this island, daring time to try to change their way of life. They lived by the ageless rhythm of the sea. We shared a cup of coffee with them and took our leave.

Just as we rounded out the walk, we came upon the Notre-Dame de la Garde hospital, a four-storey solid brick building. It was a big rectangle with a cross on top and eight windows per side. It was well kept—newly painted and without a brick out of place. The hospital was the last stop for most people on the island.

"If the sea doesn't get 'em, most folks around here will meet their Maker right here," said Grandpa.

In a way, he had almost met his Maker here too.

The Magdalen Islands were founded by shipwrecked people. Close to its shores, there have been over one hundred wrecks. It is an island of castaways. Folks from the mainland washed up onto the beaches of the island, leaving their old lives beyond the Gulf of St. Lawrence behind. They had little choice but to make a go of it on that lifeboat of land. No one was coming to look for them. Time moved on, just as the families of those who washed up there.

Ralph's father's name was Stanley MacLean. He was a carpenter, which on the Magdalen Islands meant a shipbuilder. He was a mean, violent man who belittled those around him, especially his children.

Ralph remembers one day when he was eight, his father entered the living room and strutted up to the phonograph. He put on a two-step jig. He was in a foul mood. You could feel it.

"Dance, boy," he commanded.

Ralph looked down; all he saw were two left feet. His mother had been too busy trying to put food on the table to take time to teach her second youngest son to dance. He just stood beside the couch with a bowed head.

"I can't. I got two left feet, Pa," he whispered.

Ralph was upset that he could not please his father. More than anything, he was afraid of what would happen next. He was right to be afraid.

His father used his big boot to kick Ralph into the couch. His small frame hit the couch hard, bouncing him straight back onto the hardwood floor. Violence of this sort was unpredictable. Was it a brief flash of rage that would quickly retreat into its ugly old cave? That was rarely the case, but there was always hope.

"Quit crying, boy," Stanley threatened.

Ralph knew more was to come if he didn't stop. But he just couldn't. He was eight and he was gasping. He lay on the wood floor, seeing two big boots right in front of his face, then one. The next kick propelled him to the doorway. When he landed, instinct took over. He tried to grasp the archway as he scrambled to gain his footing. That didn't work. His father's boot plowed into his lower back. He was licked. All he could do was close his eyes and curl up into a ball. It was his only hope. It took three more kicks for the storm to pass. The last kick sent him flailing right through the open patio door. Ralph lay in the mud of the backyard, bloodied and battered.

I have never seen my grandfather dance.

If Ralph's father was the darkness in his life, his mother was the light. Susan MacLean was his saving grace. Grace comes in many forms, and God works in mysterious ways. Ralph knew this through his mother. He never called her Mother. It was always "Dearest Mother," because that's what she was. When he speaks of her at length, which he often does, his Maritime accent washes ashore and mother becomes "mutter."

Susan had eight children to feed, clothe, and make right with her Lord: Irene, Ada, Arthur, Lillian, Mabel, Greta, Ralph, and Ford. Little Irene met her Lord after only two years of life. The remaining seven would read about Him every night as soon as the dinner dishes were done.

~~~~~

Ralph MacLean's very first memory was of red Mandarin writing on a storefront window. He was in Charlottetown, Prince Edward Island. The red letters were followed by his second memory: being chased by an angry Chinese launderer armed with a hot iron.

Ralph and his rascal of a little brother, Ford, had been sent to Charlottetown under the care of their eldest sister. It was their first time away from home. Their sister Ada had moved to Prince Edward Island during the winter of 1926. Ada was older and busy with her own budding family, so the boys at seven and five were largely on their own, which was just how they liked it.

On that particular day, Ada had given them each two bits and they'd bought candy bars on their way down to the shoreline. Ralph and Ford ate their chocolate by the water, which was calm that day, and skipped rocks off the wharf. On their way back to Ada's, they passed a Chinese laundry. The lettering on the window was exotic. They'd never seen anything like it. Different meant from away. Different was feared and desired. Different had a name: "chink."

"That's a chink's shop," Ford said.

Ralph wondered what *chink* meant. He'd never heard the word before. How had his kid brother got the jump on him?

"Chink!" Ford repeated for effect.

The two boys looked at each other, then turned and stared past the lettering into the shop.

A man was pressing shirts just behind the small counter while a woman swept the foyer. Neither boy had ever seen Chinese people before. They looked different than the people they were accustomed to. It was their eyes that captured Ralph's attention and prompted his imagination. He tried to figure out how these folks had got here. What did they like? Could they skate on the pond in the winter? They may as well have been aliens. Ralph was in awe. Ford was not.

An ocean breeze picked up and blew road dust into their faces. Ford squinted and spit on the wooden platform in front of the shop.

"Hey, Chinaman," he called through the open door.

The man slowly raised his head. He knew what was coming.

Ford put his little chubby fingers to his eyes and pulled them across his face. The grime behind his nails betrayed his poverty. The four people stood still, just staring at one another. Now that Ford had the man's attention, he wasn't sure what to do with it. The shop owner surely hoped that the two boys before him would simply decide they had had their fun and move on. But Ford could not help himself. At five, he'd been beaten enough to understand that the strong can force themselves on the weak. He had never been the strong. He liked turning the tables.

"You and your wife are *chinks!*"

Taking abuse from a five- and seven-year-old proved too much for the shop owner. He charged at them with the hot iron still firmly in his hand. The boys fled. Ralph hoped that the shop owner would let up, but he did not. As they ran, they glanced back to see him pass the threshold of his shop and run down the wooden platform and across the dirt road. He was yelling at them in Mandarin something terrible.

Ralph grabbed Ford's hand as they dashed past six more store-fronts, making their way to a park, where they hoped they could lose their pursuer in the trees. But as they got to the park's open space, the man gained on them with his longer legs. Ralph was hurrying Ford along when the launderer swung the hot iron, just missing his left temple. It could have been a fatal blow. Ralph had taken two more steps when his brother's hand broke away and a kick to his rear sent Ford three feet in the air. He landed on the grass and slid on his side for a few more feet. Ralph stopped running. He was the older brother. He couldn't leave Ford, however scared he was. Ford lay on his side, weeping. The launderer stood on guard, breathing heavily. Ralph made sure to stand between the two of them. He looked into the launderer's eyes, saying nothing. Then the man turned and left.

Ralph made sure the man had moved on before turning his attention back to Ford. He knew a beating isn't over until it's over. When he was sure the man wasn't coming back, Ralph kneeled and put his hand on Ford's shoulder.

"You'll be fine, Ford, he just clipped your seat. Cm'on—get up."

Ford did, and they stood staring at each other. Their minds raced. They'd spent the past four minutes being the aggressors, the victims, the bullies, and the vanquished. They both had adrenaline coursing through their veins. Ralph's knees were still shaking. He suggested they head back to Ada's. Ford suggested they head back to the beach, and flashed Ralph the same devilish smile that he would come to rely on for the rest of his days. Ford had already moved on from the experience. But Ralph had not. He felt bad about the way they had treated the man. They had insulted him, insulted his wife. At seven, he knew right and wrong. They'd done wrong that afternoon.

The only other thing Ralph remembered about that trip to Charlottetown so many years ago was the last supper that sister Ada made especially for them, a feast of mackerel and cheese. Mackerel was Ralph's favourite fish. It would be their last dinner with her for some time. The boys were leaving for home. The nine-hour ferry ride from the rich red beaches of Souris, Prince Edward Island, would take them through the Gulf of St. Lawrence, past Entry Island, to the Magdalen Islands.

A few months after their trip to Prince Edward Island, Ford came down with scarlet fever. Dr. Solomon, the island's English-speaking doctor, had to paint the dreaded red quarantine emblem on the MacLean's front door. Stanley MacLean kept walking when he was done work. To go in the house would court financial ruin for the family. Their mother was left alone to tend to Ford day and night. After three weeks, Ralph came down with it too. Their mother did not sleep for more than a few fleeting moments during the three months her two boys burned with fever. She put them on a gruel diet to keep their temperature down. Ralph emerged unscathed, but Ford's heart tissue was irreparably damaged.

The MacLeans lived in a two-storey, four-bedroom country house that Stanley had built with his own two hands. It was painted white, but the salt, the wind, the rain, and the fog had all conspired to leave it in a state of constant disrepair. Since all the houses on the island were the same, the family never felt bad about it.

They had a large garden in the back where they would grow carrots, beets, tomatoes, squash, onions, and parsnips. Behind the garden lay a small barn for the family horse, Old Jack. One day Old Jack almost killed the oldest brother, Arthur. He was taking some forty-five-gallon oil drums down to the shop of Mr. Grey, the island's Marconi operator. As Arthur hopped off Old Jack to drop off the barrels, the horse got spooked and bolted. Arthur's foot caught in his saddle and he was dragged for a half-mile. Two barrels fell on him, and he was struck once by Old Jack's hoof. Four hours later, Mr. Grey brought him home through the back patio door. Ralph did not recognize his own brother. His skin was as white as paper.

Old Jack's barn was adjacent to the family's milk-cow corral. In honour of the epic journey this cow had travelled to get there, it was named Lovat, after the boat that was the only way on or off the island. In the winter of 1930, Susan MacLean had secretly sent a tele-gram to her brother, who lived on Prince Edward Island, asking that he find it in his heart to offer Stanley a milk cow. The family needed milk and it was just getting too expensive to buy. Stanley was too proud to ask for help. Plus, the rumrunners' boats had been docked off the coast for the better part of the last month, which always had a dramatic impact on the family finances.

Money had been drawn from the family's bank account. Ralph remembers his mother crying in the kitchen one day. "The money— where has it gone?" They could see the white sails of the rum boat from the living room bay window. Seven hungry children sat at the kitchen table, not a leg among them long enough to touch the wooden floor, and they all knew exactly where the money had gone.

Thank God for the potatoes. Behind the corral and the barn lay an acre of potato patch. All nine souls in the house depended on that acre. The sea provided folks on the island with money, but potatoes kept them alive.

In May 1939, when Ralph was seventeen, his sister Mabel gave birth to a beautiful baby girl. She was named Alayne. It was the first baby for the MacLean siblings, a real reason to celebrate. Ralph's mother opened three jars of peaches that had been shipped in from Nova Scotia. The pop of the peach jar was like a champagne cork going off. The family had never seen three jars open at the same time. Everyone around the kitchen table tried their best to concentrate on the sweet nectar of the peaches, but an elephant in the room was suffocating the celebration. They were worried for this baby's father. Doug Stevens was in the thick of the war by then.

When the Germans launched the Blitzkrieg attack in 1939, Mabel's husband could not wait for his government to join the fight. He was one of the first Canadians to join Britain's Royal Air Force. Since Canada was a member of the British Commonwealth, the Brits were happy to take as many of her men as they could. Churchill knew how admirably Canadians had served during the First World War and hoped they'd do so again.

Doug Stevens saw Germany's Blitzkrieg into Poland as the first move by a harsh regime waging a brutal war inside and outside its country's borders. Doug rallied to the call. He joined the Royal Air Force in the winter of 1939 and was off to England soon thereafter. Mabel was four months pregnant. Doug hid the fact that he was married because the Brits would only take single men. They knew the odds that airmen faced. Doug trained in England and became a pilot of a mighty Lancaster bomber. He sent back a picture of himself in uniform standing at the side of his plane. Mabel set that picture up against the lamp on her nightstand. How she worried about her husband flying the skies above occupied France!

Mabel was left on her own. Her long-time friend Kay Vincent came back to the island to stay with her for most of that spring and summer. Kay had moved to Halifax a few years earlier to work in a grocery store owned by an uncle. Kay was a great help to Mabel, and to repay the favour, Mabel decided to accompany her back to Halifax in November of 1939.

At that point, Ralph didn't have much on his plate. And nobody wanted Mabel to travel on her own with a baby in tow. So he offered to accompany Kay, Mabel, and baby Alayne to Halifax. Ralph's chivalry—which had always been second nature to him—was no doubt influenced by a desire to get off the island, far from the close confines of the house, and away from lousy job offerings. Mostly, away from his father.

They boarded the SS *Lovat* and steamed off to Pictou, Prince Edward Island. The steamship had a few staterooms, though none were particularly stately. The three adults and the baby had a small bunk bed and a couch by the window, neither of which were terribly comfortable. But the room did offer some privacy and was a noise barrier between them and the other passengers. Six-month-old Alayne was colicky and inconsolable.

The Gulf of St. Lawrence is typically a rough waterway. The winds off the north Atlantic sweep through and bear down on the boats with no mercy. The trip across the straight was plagued by these fierce winds. At night, Mabel was able to get Alayne down to sleep on the bottom bunk, so Ralph slipped up to the top bunk to try to get a few hours of rest before the baby woke again. In the middle of his slumber, Ralph was thrown out of his bunk with great force. He awoke in a standing position in the middle of the stateroom, staring into the dark. There was an eerie silence on the ship. The engine had stopped completely. He could hear only the wind and the water lashing up against the metal hull. Alayne somehow slept on. Ralph feared that the ship had hit something or a U-boat had hit them. A flash of panic came over him as he stood there in silence, at attention, waiting for something to react to.

Mabel sat up on the lower bunk and Kay awoke on the couch. They all waited in silence.

Whoosh, whoosh, whoosh, they heard. Water was swirling around the vessel.

Kay whispered, "Are we sinking?"

Mabel scrambled to her feet, instinctively snatching Alayne from the bed and clutching her. Kay joined them and they huddled together around their main protector—a skinny seventeen-year-old boy. Finally, the engines roared back to life. A wave had pushed the bow so high that the rudders had come clear out of the water and tripped off. As her fear subsided, Mabel mentioned that she had not heard Ralph get out of bed. This would not be the last time my grandfather landed—miraculously—on his feet.

When they arrived in Pictou, Ralph said he hoped he would not see the SS *Lovat* again for some time.

They boarded a train to Truro to visit the McArthurs, who had left the Magdalen Islands a few years back to set up a cattle farm. The McArthurs had done well and had enough room to comfortably put up the four visitors. Ralph sent word back home that they had arrived in Pictou almost without incident and were en route to Truro, where they would be staying for the next week or so. Alayne was especially colicky and Mabel was happy to rest for a little while.

They all sat down to a beautiful meal of roast beef with Yorkshire pudding, caramelized carrots, and creamy whipped P.E.I. potatoes. (Ralph was a connoisseur of the humble potato.) Mr. McArthur asked Ralph if he'd like to bless the meal. Ralph already had his hands joined above his empty plate.

"Dear Jesus," he said, "thank you for this food, bless it to our bodies. Thank you for our safe travels and for the time we can all spend together. Dear Jesus, bless our little Alayne. Keep her safe and bless her father. Please keep Douglas safe over Europe's skies. In your name, we pray. Amen."

"Amen," the table responded in unison.

With that, they dug into the meal with a clanging of utensils, passing of serving dishes, offers to pass the salt, the milk, the butter, more potatoes, and praises to the cook. The night ended with a game of cards, but the prayer was needed. The next day would be the most difficult of Mabel's life.

Ralph woke to his favourite breakfast, a soft-boiled egg with butter, salt, and pepper. Mrs. McArthur placed a cup of Scottish breakfast tea in front of him. He was still in his pyjamas, with a borrowed housecoat to cut the November morning chill. When he heard a knock at the front door, he instinctively stood up to answer, but Mrs. McArthur put her hand on his shoulder and told him she'd get it.

The opened door ushered in a wave of cool, damp air. A cold front had moved in overnight. Ralph heard a man's voice ask for

Mabel Stevens. Who would be looking for Mabel here? The only person who knew they were there was his mother. And then it hit him like an ocean surge.

Ralph didn't need to read the telegram in the messenger's hand. He knew what it said. He slowly got to his feet and went upstairs. He put his ear to the door of the room where Mabel slept. He heard Alayne cooing, so he knew Mabel must be awake. He knocked and cracked the door open.

"Mabel, there is a messenger here for you."

Ralph knew this was the sentence she had been dreading since Douglas left her arms. He could see she was paralyzed with dread. He helped her sit up on the side of the bed. Alayne continued to coo as he scrambled to find a wool shawl for Mabel to throw over her shoulders in the room's half-light. He helped her to her feet and quickly swaddled Alayne.

As they made their way down the stairs, Mabel turned to her brother. "I can't do this, Ralph. I just . . . I just can't bear it."

"Lean on me, dear. Let's do this together."

Mabel really *couldn't* do it. The sight of the messenger was too much. He was Death. Her legs gave out. Ralph passed Alayne to Mrs. McArthur and picked his sister up—propped her up—to take the shock of the news.

"Mrs. Stevens, I regret to inform you that your husband, Douglas Stevens, died in a plane crash. He died in service. Please accept my condolences and this message from the Royal Air Force."

With that, the messenger bowed his head and offered a final "I'm sorry" as Mrs. McArthur closed the door. The foyer was freezing but Mabel seemed completely unaware. Her knees buckled once again and this time Ralph eased her to the ground. He sat beside her, rubbing her back. She was motionless, silent. Finally, as if the weight of the news had just then hit her, Mabel let out a frightful moan. It was deep, low, and sorrowful, and it came up from the pit of her stomach. She was in the middle of a hell that abandons all reality, all manners, all social graces. Mabel lay on that landing for over an hour. She wailed, trembled, and sobbed herself into a state of sheer exhaustion. Ralph stayed at her side on the cold floor. Blankets were offered but Mabel eschewed them. She sought no comfort. She knew there was none to be had.

She and Alayne were alone.

That afternoon, Ralph sent word to his mother and to the Stevens family. Mr. and Mrs. Stevens had already heard the news and had gleaned additional bits of information from telegrams from Douglas's friend, who had been serving with him in Great Britain.

Douglas's squad had been training for night-bombing runs into France. He had gone up with a group of Wellingtons over the English Channel. His plane malfunctioned and he and his co-pilot struggled to make it home. They almost made it.

As Douglas's comrades landed and were getting out of their planes, they saw his screaming into a hillside cliff, a thick trail of black smoke behind it. An emergency crew recovered his plane and he was found in the cockpit, still strapped in. He hadn't ejected. He had never given up on getting his buddies home safely. Douglas Stevens was buried in Uxbridge, England.

Ralph promised Mr. Stevens that he would have Mabel call him as soon as she was able. He hung up the phone, went to his sister, and picked up her limp body. She was long beyond being hysterical. She was beyond anything. Ralph took her back up to the bed where he'd found her a mere hour ago—a lifetime ago.

He returned downstairs and kneeled beside Alayne's bassinet and listened to her coo. This little soul would never know the pain of the moment—there would be no scars. She would only come to know this day by the emptiness it would leave in its wake. She would never feel the warm, deep hug that only a father can provide. Ralph cried for Alayne that afternoon. He cried for her, and he cried for Mabel. He cried for himself.

The next morning Mabel emerged from her room seared by loss. It would never leave her eyes. She never really got up from the landing. She went somewhere for those few hours. The experience pierced her and took something from her. Some things you just can't ever get back.

As Ralph had promised, Mabel called Douglas's family. She sat at the table and he stood beside her, his hand on her shoulder, as she picked up the phone and dialled the number. "It's Mabel . . . yes . . . well, I'm doing better now . . . the baby? . . . She's fine . . . sleeping now . . . I can . . . okay . . . I will. Mr. Stevens, thank you. I'll see you soon." With that, Mabel hung up the phone and bowed her head.

Ralph gave her time. She blew her nose, wiped her eyes, and looked up at her brother.

"Mr. Stevens said, 'Mabel, you come to us,'" she reported, crying tears of gratefulness.

Two days later, Ralph bundled up Alayne and saw her and his sister off on the train. Mabel was taking up the Stevens' invitation. She would stay with them for three years. Alayne's father would never hold her, but her grandfather was there for her. At the Stevens's, Mabel and Alayne recovered. There, Alayne grew.

On his own now, Ralph struck out for Halifax, where he would be staying with his sister Greta, who worked at the harbour magazine depot. Walking down Front Street with his suitcase to catch the train, he got it in his mind to follow Douglas's footsteps into battle. Revenge was in his heart. The war had hit his family and he was never one to back down from a fight: not from the Downroaders, not from his dad, and certainly not from the Nazis. As with most of life's major decisions, there was no fanfare, no fireworks. There was just Ralph MacLean walking down Front Street. He took the train and got off at the Pier 21 exit, then he hiked up Water Street and went to the docks. He walked into the naval recruitment station.

There, Ralph was told the damnedest thing he'd ever heard.

"Sorry, son," said the naval official, "we are just taking boys from the Prairies."

The Prairies?

Ralph looked around the room. He didn't see a single fellow who looked like he was from the Prairies.

He pleaded his case: "I'm fit to serve, sir. I know my way around a boat."

He made sure to make eye contact with the official.

"I want to fight." Not much more could be said.

"I don't doubt any of that, son. But I got my orders. We're only taking men from the Prairies. I'm sorry. Come back in a few months," the official said, making it clear the conversation was over.

With nothing more to do, Ralph nodded, picked up his suitcase, and left the building. Shoulders slumped, he trudged along the boardwalk.

"Prairie boys," he mumbled to himself, still shocked.

After visiting with Greta for a few days, he decided to go home to Grindstone. He didn't really want to, but he didn't seem to have much choice. He was flat broke and, not being from the Prairies, was of no use to the Navy. He wired his buddy Deighton Aitken, who came to pick him up at the island dock.

The two friends spent a few weeks celebrating. Deighton had spent much of the last summer out at sea and had had several good hauls of mackerel and lobster. Unlike Ralph, he had money in his pocket. They spent the next few weeks in and out of various rum bottles.

Life went on like that for some time. They'd pick up odd jobs, make enough to run around with, find another job when they ran out of money. As the spring turned to summer, both grew tired of this routine. They were restless. They could feel the grass growing under their feet on that tiny island and they both sought adventures. They wanted to do something—anything—with their lives. And Ralph still had the gnawing of revenge in his heart. The summer wore on and their restlessness grew more intense. They would go from house to house, visiting friends, drinking beer, all the while growing more frustrated with their station in life.

On the night of August 25, 1940, Deighton knocked on the back door of Ralph's house. They had a routine night of gin rummy planned with Lloyd and Ada Geddes, long-time neighbours of the MacLeans. Lloyd Geddes had a way with cards—but a terrible sense of humour. After a couple of hours of stiff drinks and crummy jokes, Deighton kicked Ralph under the table. That was the cue to leave. They finished the hand, thanked Ada for the hospitality, and made a quick exit.

They walked down the main road, hands in pockets, kicking small pebbles along the gravel road. Deighton raised his collar to shield himself from the sea breeze. Ralph didn't seem to notice. His mind was elsewhere.

"You know, Ralphie, a team of chaps came today recruiting from *Quee-bec*. I hear they are looking to fill two regiments full of men: one English and one French. That's a couple thousand men they're looking for—just from around these parts alone. They've been through the Eastern Townships and they're fixin' to make their way straight through to Nova Scotia's South Shore."

Ralph tried to keep his cool. "Oh yeah, where have they set up shop on the island?"

"The hospital."

"Well, whatdya think?" Ralph asked—knowing full well what Deighton thought.

"Might be worth heading down there and takin' a look-see."

"God knows, I can't take another night of Lloyd's jokes," Ralph said.

"Okay then, we'll go first thing tomorrow. I'll pick you up after breakfast."

Ralph spent that night dreaming of gallivanting around Europe with his buddy Deighton. They could see the world. They could see the world's women. He'd be far away from Lloyd's jokes, his father's insults, and the mundane jobs he was picking up. He'd have a uniform, a gun, and a duty to discharge. He'd have purpose.

The next morning Ralph watched the sunrise from the back door step. Deighton arrived soon after, and together they went to the hospital. Neither of them had discussed this move with their families. They had decided—together—to enlist.

Walking up the hill towards the hospital they saw a group of chaps loitering around the entrance. Inside the hospital, recruitment was an orderly affair. There were two tables in the main foyer and a Canadian flag pinned up behind them on the wall. The green Royal Rifles of Canada—unfamiliar to Ralph—hung on a portable flagpole. The insignia read: *Volens et valens*. The Latin was lost on them both. A recruiting officer pointed to the unfamiliar words as he translated: "Willing and able."

At the table on the left sat a man with a buzz cut and a clipboard. Ralph took his turn with the officer.

"What's your name, son?"

Ralph examined the army badge on the officer's shoulder, the First World War medal for something or other, the sidearm.

"Son, what's your name?" the officer repeated.

"Ralph Augustus MacLean, sir," he offered, standing as he guessed a soldier should stand.

"Live here in Grindstone?"

"Yes sir, just down the ways above Splendid Beach."

"Age?" The officer's face was buried in the clipboard.

"I'm eighteen, sir."

"When were you born, son?"

"1922."

"The date. What day were you born?"

"June 27, 1922."

"You've only been eighteen for two months then, huh? Well, we're going to have to change that."

Ralph flashed the office a confused look.

"Son, you can't go overseas until you are nineteen. So we need to fix your birthdate if you're going to go overseas with your buddy here."

Ralph and Deighton looked at each other; Deighton flashed his toothy grin. Ralph nodded.

"There, that's better," the officer said as a few scratches of a pencil aged Ralph ten months.

The officer waved his hand and gave them both a *we're in on it* smile.

"We're done here, gents. Go to the next table."

The two buddies sat side by side on chairs at the next table and signed what was put in front of them. That was that. Rifleman Ralph Augustus MacLean. E30382. Headquarters Company. 4 Carrier MD5 Platoon. Over time he'd shout that combination of words and numbers to more drill officers than he could count. He'd whisper it once with a sword at his throat.

Both Ralph and Deighton were riflemen in the Royal Rifles of Canada, 1st Battalion. In two weeks, they were to be shipped to Valcartier, Quebec, for basic training.

CHAPTER 2

Cast Away

My grandma was born Mitsue Oseki. She was her family's first-born daughter. In Japanese families, the eldest daughter is called *ne-san*. Her brothers and sisters called her Nenny for short. That name stuck, and to this day, the ones who are still alive call her Nenny. Their kids, and their kids' kids, call her Aunty Nenny.

Her name, Mitsue, means Shining Branch. Her father gave her the name because her parents and those that came before them were the roots and the trunk of the tree. They grounded her and gave her life. And as the eldest, she was to support them in turn, to keep the tree alive and well, to grow. She tried her best.

Mitsue was born on June 10, 1920, in Eburne, British Columbia. She was born Canadian. She was lucky to be born into the home of Yosuke and Tomi Oseki.

Yosuke and Tomi had a special kind of relationship, ahead of their time, founded on mutual respect, rooted in love. The two of them would speak late into the night, holding hands across the kitchen table. They had a lot to discuss. Neither had anticipated living across the Pacific Ocean from their land, away from Japan and their beloved families.

Yosuke was a second son. He was not responsible for the family's land in Chiba the way his older brother was. He wanted to venture out and see the world. Yosuke thought long and hard about what business opportunities he might be able to explore that would be of interest to his fellow countrymen. He came up with two things: beef and shoes.

In 1907, Canadian officials in Japan were taking names of men who wanted to obtain Dominion visas. Yosuke did not know much about Canada, but he did know that Canada had a lot of cows and that everyone wore shoes. That was enough for him. He signed up and was one of the first men chosen.

Yosuke left Japan in search of brighter days. He cast off from his beloved island with a heavy but hopeful heart. He was leaving as dark clouds were forming over the Land of the Rising Sun. He felt the poison in the air.

The Vancouver that Yosuke Oseki fled to in 1907 was a pioneer town—muddy, rainy, hardscrabble. The Japanese all congregated along Powell Street. The name of that part of town was as unwelcoming as the country: "Japtown." It was so isolated from the broader Vancouver community that it may as well have been in Japan. There, the first-generation Japanese—the *Issei*—huddled together to shield themselves from their strange and generally hostile new surroundings. They tried their best to recreate their lives. Tastes and traditions brought them comfort. Merchants made tofu and imported rice, tea, and sake. Four square blocks of fishmongers, boarding houses, dry cleaners, grocers, and *izakaya* houses formed the epicentre of the Japanese experience in Canada. While almost all of the immigrants were literate, it was in the Japanese language. Most did not speak English, but the safety and security of Japantown allowed them to function with ease.

By 1907, nearly eight thousand of the Emperor's subjects were living in Canada—and these were, almost to the last soul, in British Columbia. But the welcome mat was not out. The media portrayed these eight thousand, and their Chinese counterparts, as the "Asian invasion" and the "yellow peril." Several high-profile politicians capitalized on the public's resentment and fear. Hate groups such as the Asiatic Expulsion League migrated north from the United States. Ruthlessness ruled the day. National newspapers printed venom in black and white that aimed to strip Asian residents of their very humanity. They were, in large part, successful.

Unemployment was high, and blame had to fall somewhere. Idle hands so easily turned into active fists. On September 7, an angry mob took their hostility to the street in Canada's first race riot. Close to ten thousand men gathered around City Hall. The mob was determined to spend the evening ridding Vancouver of the "Japs" and "Chinks." *Stand for a White Canada* banners waved above heads as the crowd marched through Chinatown smashing every window in sight.

As the mob turned the corner onto Powell Street to do the same in Little Tokyo, the Japanese men readied themselves. They had learned about what was happening around Carrall Street. They heard the mob march like an army. Everyone turned out their lights. The women and children hid wherever they could. The men were on the roofs, waiting. There was no time to prepare, and no speeches were made, but everyone knew that they were going to defend themselves. They had families, and the mob was violent. There were some police, but they did little to stop the mob from advancing.

As the mob neared, the Japanese men began throwing stones down from their rooftops. This slowed the mob's progress, but soon those same rocks were going through store windows and the Japanese had to charge with anything they had: sticks, knifes, more rocks.

Fierce hand-to-hand combat erupted on Powell Street. Bloodied bodies littered the street. There were gunshots. The fight went on throughout the night. Shopkeepers and miners became sentries. Fishermen became medics. The Japanese defended their neighbourhood with an intensity not anticipated by the mob. Men, five at a time, would charge at a dozen men twice their size. It should not have been much a fight, but it was. By dawn, the Japanese had successfully defended their beloved Powell Street, although not without significant casualties. Bandaged men littered the sidewalks. It looked like it had hailed shards of glass. Bodies were battered, stores and homes were damaged, but the Japanese were not defeated. They held their bloodied heads high.

In response to pressure from the Canadian government, Japan agreed to restrict the number of passports issued for Canada to a mere four hundred per year. And there it was: the first action against Japanese Canadians. The tiniest of steps. History has proven all too many times that discrimination in any form is a downward spiral.

Like most Japanese men, Yosuke fished. He was very good at it, he always seemed to find where the fish were. He would spend the evening looking at maps, tracing his finger over the rivers and inlets along the coast, tapping the map when he found his spot. He would whisper to himself at the kitchen table. He was almost praying, or maybe he *was* praying. His family needed him to catch fish, but they never worried. They knew he would. And he always did, until he couldn't.

The Oseki family had moved from Eburne, a farming community between Vancouver and Richmond, to a Vancouver neighbourhood known as Celtic right after Mitsue was born because Toru, the eldest son, had just turned seven and Eburne did not have a school for him. Even at seven, Toru understood the position he held. Tradition dictated that he would be the one taking care of the family. He took his responsibilities seriously.

Eichi, the second son, had his father's build. As a young child, he was teased a little because of his round shape. So instead of calling him fat, Toru called him Pat. It made Eichi feel better. The name stuck and he was called Pat all his life.

Even when Pat was a young boy, it was clear he had inherited his dad's fishing instincts. He was every bit as precise. He could always find the best place to fish, and he spent his whole life doing it. Mitsue never saw a better fisherman than her brother Pat.

In the spring of 1926, Yosuke got a job with a cannery in Celtic and moved his growing family into one of the company houses just off 49th Street, south of Brennan Street. They were row houses, eight per row. Each house had three wooden steps that led to a framed front door with a window and a flowerbox on either side. The house was small but warm and comfortable.

When Yosuke was home, he would gather the family around the front sitting room and talk. He made sure they always talked as a family and he led sessions that would go on for hours. Whenever a big decision was to be made, he would sit everyone down in that room. There was not enough space on the couch for them all, so he would bring in a kitchen chair to sit on. He would listen to his family and challenge them to consider issues in different ways. He'd then deliberate on what he had heard, and, when he was ready, tell them what he thought they should do. Yosuke's familial behaviour was exceptional for a Japanese man. He had a mind for thinking things through. He kept things close to his heart.

There were two bedrooms off the living room. Tomi and Yosuke slept in one with the girls, and the boys slept in the other. Mitsue shared a bed with her sister Mary, while the baby, Susanne, had a small bed beside theirs. The kitchen was in the back of the house. There was an outhouse in the backyard near the garden. A few years after they moved in, Yosuke built a bathroom off the kitchen and had a Japanese soaker tub put in. A fire had to be lit under the tub to keep the water warm. Visiting friends marvelled at how prosperous Yosuke was. The house even had running water and electricity.

The secret to Yosuke's success was his two fishing licences. He could fish for both salmon in the summer and cod in the winter. None of his friends had two licences. Most of them could fish for salmon, but not for cod. Yosuke had thought it through. He could fish year-round. But the extra income came at a price.

There were only a few cod licences granted to Japanese men. It was the cod that took Yosuke out to sea from February through to May, to fish around Pender Island. He'd have no rest and his family would miss him desperately—his talks, his warmth, his calm. But they did not want for anything. Though they didn't have a lot, they always had what they needed.

Yosuke had two boats: one for salmon and one for cod. The salmon boat was smaller because he used it just for the day, but the cod boat was much bigger. Cod fishing was especially tough. The weather was cold and the days were long. When Yosuke docked for the evening, he would read all night. He always took the Bible out to sea with him, and the Buddhist teachings.

Mitsue loved the summer because the salmon fishing was good. From May until September, Yosuke would fish the Fraser River. In those days, the salmon was close, so Yosuke would be home every night. He'd catch all kinds of salmon: sockeye, coho, pink, white springs, and chum. Sockeye was the best, and made him the most money, but Mitsue loved it when her dad caught chum because they salted it and made *ochazuke*. She loved how the salted fish tasted in the hot rice. Tomi would add a plum *umeboshi* to make it a little sweet and sour. Tomi, Mitsue, and Mary would bone, salt, and dry mountains of chum. On those summer nights, the Celtic families would throw potluck feasts and all the women would bring their sushi and chow mein. The men would bring their fishing tales.

The commercial success that paid for the life Mitsue was living had ramifications. There was no matter of greater contention than the success of the Japanese in the B.C. fishing industry. The Japanese had come to Canada ready to fish. They had generations' worth of experience and were exceptionally skilled. By 1925, Japanese were bringing in the biggest hauls in the country. They were prospering in their new home. This did not go unnoticed.

Toru was a fine brother to Mitsue. Her eyes danced when she reflected on him. She sat on the edge of her seat when he spoke.

In Celtic, Toru's position as the eldest son was more than symbolic. It transcended the Japanese way of life. The Pacific's winter waters would take Yosuke away for months at a time. This left Toru responsible for his mother and siblings. Every day, Toru would take Mitsue to school on his bike. This was an onerous task. Mitsue had three friends that lived in the same bank of Celtic cannery row houses: Miyoko, Sumiko, and Haruko. Mitsue and Miyoko, in particular, were inseparable. Toru would deliver them all to school, shuttling each girl individually a distance up the road, only to double back and scoop up another until they had all been dropped off at school. The four girls giggled the entire two-mile trek.

At Kerrisdale Elementary School, Mitsue and Miyoko were the only Japanese kids in their grade. Sumiko and Haruko were the only other Japanese children in the school, which went up to Grade 6.

Mitsue lived in two worlds. There was the Japanese world, her community in Celtic. Her family, her friends, the food she loved, and the Japanese Centre were all there. That was the world of the familiar, filled with love. But tomorrow was not there. Mitsue knew from a very early age that her future was in the English world, the world of education, modern lifestyle, modern fads. It had movies and fashion and it spoke English. She wanted to be a part of that world. Her parents wanted her to be a part of that world too. She tried to fit in. She was taught to play by the rules, follow the instructions, and not cause any trouble. If she did well, she thought, she would be accepted.

As the eldest sister, Mitsue bore a lot of responsibility at home. Her mother depended on her. Tomi was a smart, feisty woman. She had had lots of schooling. She loved to study. When she finished grade school in Japan, she had planned to go to college to become a teacher. But her mother told her if she had too much education no man would marry her, so she didn't go. That had always saddened Mitsue.

There were a lot of chores that needed to be done to keep the family going—especially when Yosuke was out fishing. Mary was just a few years younger than Mitsue; Susanne was seven years younger. Mitsue loved to help her mother with the ironing. She would iron all of her sisters' dresses and her brothers' shirts and slacks. Everything was washed by hand and all the ironing was done on the stove.

Once a week, a truck from one of the Powell Street stores would come to Celtic. It sold all kinds of Japanese food: *nasubi*, *bok choy*, tofu, rice, *shoyu*, and *mirin*. There was never a shortage of Japanese food.

Yosuke and several of his friends rallied to try to make working conditions and pay more equitable for the Japanese fishermen. When on land, Yosuke would go door-to-door trying to convince his fellow fishermen to sell their catch at market rates. If they stuck together, he'd argue, they'd get a fair shake. Some listened, but most didn't. The concept of fairness seemed out of their grasp.

Yosuke tried to make life easier for his community and Mitsue tried to make life easier for him. The focus of family life was to assist and to be obedient, to make their parents proud. The sense of duty was constant.

On the weekends, all the siblings would go to Celtic's community park, three blocks down Brennan Street. It had an open grass field, and those old enough would play soccer or baseball. Mitsue liked soccer best because she had longer legs than most of the girls and could run faster. The Japanese kids would stick together on the weekends, rarely playing with the white children. Mitsue and Miyoko would play with the *hakujin* kids at school, but once they were on our own, they would usually stick together. There were no signs to make it official, no physical barriers; it was just the way it was.

Celtic had a Japanese centre right around the corner from the row houses, a one-storey building with two rooms that the cannery had helped build. This small building was the centre of the Japanese community's world. It was their Japanese school, their church, and the place they'd all gather for events and festivals. The parents pooled their money to pay a teacher to come every weekday from four until five to teach the children Japanese reading and writing.

After Japanese school, Mitsue, Mary, and their brothers would walk back home and have dinner with the family. Tomi was an exceptional cook. She loved to make *kamaboko* from the fish that Yosuke brought home. Mitsue would help her bone the fish and pound it in a bowl to make the fishcake. She would taste the fish to make sure it was seasoned just so, never using a recipe. She learned from her mother that every dish was a work in progress.

On the weekend they had more school. They were Japanese, after all. They would spend all day Saturday at the Japanese centre and then be back in the same building for church on Sunday morning. Mitsue was baptized there when she was sixteen, along with Miyoko, Sumiko, and Haruko. They had a Baptist minister, a wonderful man named Mr. Harry who drove in with his wife and three children from Kerrisdale. Mr. Harry and his family were the only white people in the entire congregation.

Mitsue and Miyoko graduated to Point Grey Junior High School in the fall of 1932. They were still the only Japanese girls in their grade. They both excelled. By Grade 9, their families had a decision to make: should the girls go on to high school? Yosuke and Tomi had never doubted this. Mitsue and Miyoko went on to Magee Secondary School.

All the other Celtic parents decided against further education for their daughters. Eight years seemed plenty for a Japanese girl in 1932. So while Magee was a much larger school than Mitsue and Miyoko had ever attended, they encountered even fewer Japanese students than before. Gone were the days of hitching a ride on Toru's bicycle. Her brother had graduated with honours. Mitsue wished he were there. She felt she was about to need him.

She was right.

One morning in November, for the first time, Miyoko was not waiting out front of Mitsue's door to go to school. Nor the next morning. Nor the next. A family meeting was called. Mitsue walked into the living room, her belly in knots.

"Miyoko is getting the test," Tomi announced, her eyes squarely on Mitsue. Everyone knew what *the test* was. No further explanation was needed. Tuberculosis was everywhere. If you got it, you were in peril.

Mitsue was frightened. What if she had TB? Could she have passed it on to her family? Tomi took Mitsue for the same test.

Miyoko's test results came back. She had TB. She was immediately taken to the sanatorium, where nobody could visit. Everyone just waited and hoped—and prayed—for the best. Mitsue knew her timid friend was scared in that big, cold building without relatives or friends. But Mitsue didn't fret for long; Miyoko died within the week.

Mitsue could not go to her best friend's funeral. She was waiting for her own test results. She never got to say goodbye. Her test results came back and she was fine. The next day she returned to school—now the only Japanese girl in her grade.

Mitsue felt her loneliness every morning as she opened her front door. It walked with her to the train. It sat beside her in class. Only Toru made her smile.

Toru was eighteen and had graduated from Magee. Yosuke wanted Toru to go on to college straightaway, but Toru didn't know what to study. So Yosuke took his eldest son out cod fishing for the season so he could earn some money. They could discuss his future on those long nights on the boat.

Only four weeks into the season, Yosuke arrived back home. He sat on the small porch for hours. He was physically unable to go into the house with the news he had. When Tomi opened the door and saw her husband sitting there, she fell to her knees. She knew something was terribly wrong. Yosuke had never come home early before.

Another family meeting was called. Mitsue had never before seen her father shed a tear. He could only utter a few words. Toru was in the hospital. He had fallen ill on the open waters.

The family visited Toru in the hospital. He was pale and drenched in sweat. The relatives lingered, unable to help. Toru died two days later. Nobody knew what had caused his death. He was buried in Mountain View Cemetery on Fraser Street. Nobody spoke at his funeral. There was nothing they could say.

Mitsue tried to be strong. She was the *ne-san*. She cried when she was alone, washing the dishes or getting ready for bed. She cried on the train to school. She cried on the walk home.

No one in the family got over Toru. Time does not heal all.

In the spring of that year, Mitsue started teaching Sunday school at the Celtic centre. This was a godsend for her. It delivered her from her constant sadness. The children and the bible stories soothed her and brought peace into her heart. Every Sunday, she would teach five little girls and one boy. They would begin at 9 a.m., when the preacher was with the adults in the room next door. They'd have singalongs and then read from the Bible. Mitsue came to love those children, and they her. Those six children were like candles that illuminated Mitsue through the darkness cast by Toru's death.

Mitsue emerged from her pain at that certain age when boys were starting to come around. Pat was her eldest brother now, and he ran around with a crew of Celtic boys. He and Mitsue would go out driving in his Model T Ford. Mitsue would bring Sumiko and Haruko, wishing Miyoko were there too. Pat kept that old car going against all odds. He was as good a mechanic as he was a fisherman. They'd drive to the beach and spend the day by the water. Mitsue would swim if the weather was warm. She loved the way the water felt, always cool and refreshing. Looking out into the distance, she'd think of her father and always whisper a prayer for his safety. Fishing was such a dangerous way to make a living.

After high school, Mitsue attended dressmaking school. When she was twenty, she finished her classes and started looking for a job. Since she wasn't married, she would give some money to her parents and have some spending money too. She looked around Little Tokyo for dressmaking work, and at first she didn't have much luck. But there was one storefront that had a Help Wanted sign in Japanese and English, so she went in. The store was right in the shadow of Granville Bridge. The woman who owned it was very nice and not much older than Mitsue. Her name was Mrs. Yamamoto. Mitsue showed her some of the work she had done in school and Mrs. Yamamoto hired her on the spot. Mitsue was to start every morning at eight-thirty and work until a little after five.

Mrs. Yamamoto was very kind to Mitsue, almost like a sister. She missed her own family in Japan. She had an older brother in British Columbia but he was off logging on Vancouver Island and they hardly ever saw each other. Mrs. Yamamoto had been educated in Japan and English was still difficult for her, making it hard to help the *hakujin* customers. She liked that Mitsue enjoyed all aspects of her work. She loved to sew. She could make patterns quickly and had fun with the wide selection of cloth and prints that Mrs. Yamamoto stocked. Unlike in dressmaking school, which had offered limited fabrics, here Mitsue could make dresses of all sorts, and when there was extra material Mrs. Yamamoto would let her take it home to sew something for herself. Mitsue made all her own clothes, as well as clothes for her sisters and mother. It was a labour of love.

Every night when she got off the streetcar at Brennan Street, one of Pat's friends would be waiting for her. She and her escort would walk the two miles home. With each trip, her escort would build up the confidence to propose marriage. The first man to do so was Takatsugi, whom everyone just called Tak, a nice-looking man and a very close friend of Pat's. Tak had been Mitsue's neighbour for most of her life. Of all Pat's friends, he was the one she was the most fond of.

One night Mitsue worked late at the dress shop. She didn't arrive at Brennan Street until well after 8. Tak had been waiting there for over two hours. As soon as he saw Mitsue, he approached her and blurted out that he wanted to marry her. Mitsue did not hesitate; she turned him down. They kept walking. Tak was quiet at first and then he started to cry. They walked six blocks with him in tears.

He said over and over, "Why, why, why? Why not?"

Mitsue tried to comfort him. "It's just strange for me, Tak. You're like a brother. I'm sorry, but I have to say no."

One down. Three to go.

Next Motoharu proposed. Then Minoru. Finally Ichiro. That was every one of Pat's close friends. They all asked her the exact same way—walking home on Brennan Street, just a little after six o'clock.

After each proposal, Mitsue would go home and tell Pat. He would always shake his head and say the same thing: he was sorry and he would speak to them all again.

But it didn't matter what Pat said to them. He could not deter his friends. Almost weekly, Mitsue would receive a renewed proposal. The boys would not give up. They asked over and over.

Everyone has that "one that got away." Mitsue had four. The men in her life were attracted to her beauty, to be sure. It was a particular kind of beauty. You could see your whole life in it.

Then, on a sunny spring morning, a clean-cut, well-dressed man stepped into the dress shop. His name was Hideo Sakamoto. Mitsue was expecting him. Earlier that day, Mrs. Yamamoto had told her that a schoolmate from Kumamoto prefecture in Japan would be coming by for a visit.

When the man walked into the shop, he bowed and spoke warmly to Mrs. Yamamoto. It was clear they were good friends. He was a nice-looking man with an easy, honest smile. He was polite and well-mannered, even though he was in the lumber industry. The men in that field gambled and smoked and lived away from women, so most were too rough for Mitsue's liking. Hideo was different—he was almost gentle. He was also well educated. Mitsue could tell that right away. He even came in with a book under his arm. Mitsue liked that.

Hideo worked in a paper mill, so he wasn't around Vancouver much. He had to take a boat to get to the mill and it took some time, so he would only come in to Vancouver when he had a day off, and he didn't get too many. Hideo's parents operated a rooming house in Japantown, so he would stay with them as much as he could. His visits became more frequent after he met Mitsue.

The next time Hideo came to town, after cleaning himself up

at his parents' he went straight to the store. He had asked Mrs. Yamamoto beforehand if he could take Mitsue for a walk. She had agreed, even though there was lots of work to be done.

Hideo and Mitsue went for a walk around the Granville Island Bridge. They didn't go far—Mitsue was thinking about the work that was waiting—but it was long enough. They walked a little closer than two strangers might. Mitsue could see that Hideo's hands were clean and his hair was recently cut. He wore a suit and a new white shirt, a blue-striped tie, and suspenders. His clothes were freshly pressed. But it was his warm, honest smile that she liked the best. As they rounded the corner to the dress shop, Hideo told Mitsue that he would be back in a few weeks and would like to see her again. Mitsue said that would be nice.

She spent the next two weeks hoping time would go a little faster. The days finally passed. Hideo came into the store around closing time. They walked around Hastings Street. It was a busy summer day and all the shops and restaurants were open. A photographer took a picture of them walking side by side and Hideo bought it. They stopped for a soda on Hastings Street. It was July 12, 1941: their first date.

It is clear in every picture of the two of them why my grandma was drawn to my grandpa: he simply adored her. He put her on a pedestal the height of Mount Fuji. He absolutely beamed walking down the street with her.

Hideo's easy smile did not betray Vancouver's political climate. The deep-seated racism that led to the 1907 riots had not dissipated. On the contrary; as Japanese fishermen continued to prosper, the resentment only grew. The perpetrators of hate had altered their tactics. The pen was proving mightier than the sword.

The news in the paper was all bad—but it seemed far away from Mitsue and her life. She was just working and waiting for Hideo to visit. She longed for their walks. When he was in town, he'd take the train home with her to Celtic—much to the dismay of Tak, Minoru, Motoharu, and Ichiro.

Hideo had been born in Canada, but his parents sent him to Japan in 1920, when he was six. He grew up on the family farm in Kumamoto prefecture. He knew his grandparents better than his parents. He didn't get to know his father until he came back to Canada when he was seventeen. His father was always working in the lumber mill. His mother would travel to Japan every other year to see how her son was progressing.

Hideo always retained his thick Japanese accent. Mitsue would come to feel that it held him back in life. He had a sharp intellect and read voraciously—history, geography, politics, and ecology, and he had a particular fascination with health. He read health and diet books well before they were popular. Every morning, he ate one carrot, two tomatoes, and a bowl of rice. The carrot, he thought, would keep him away from the doctors. (When my grandpa was ninety-two, I took him to his family physician in Medicine Hat for treatment for gout. The doctor sat down and just stared at him. He was in awe. He had not seen his ninety-two-year-old patient in over a decade. He turned to me and cautioned: "Kid, with genes like this, you'd better be stashing money away somewhere.")

Mitsue's father took an immediate liking to Hideo. He appreciated his intelligence. They both loved to read and they would talk about Japanese history, trading books back and forth. This was important to Mitsue. She needed her parents' blessing, especially her father's, in order to marry.

For the next few months Hideo would escort Mitsue home every day that he was not working. They got to know each other on trains, on walks through parks, and in her parent's Celtic living room.

Government repression crept into their third date, during the spring of 1941. The government ordered all Canadians of Japanese descent to obtain registration cards. It was the beginning of the end for Japanese Canadians in British Columbia. Hideo did not want to comply, but failure to do so would have resulted in jail time. He and Mitsue went to the RCMP office to register together.

The registration card included a photo, an identification number, and a fingerprint. Mitsue hated getting her fingerprints taken. She felt like a criminal. But she smiled for the camera so as not to be rude. Mitsue's card was white because she had been born in Canada; her parents' cards were pink because they had been issued Canadian citizenship. Those who were not Canadian citizens got yellow cards.

In November, Hideo worked up the nerve to speak to Yosuke. They met at the family home while Mitsue was at work. Hideo told Yosuke that he loved Mitsue and that he wanted her family's blessing and her hand in marriage. He pledged to Yosuke that he would always provide for his daughter and be by her side.

He had no idea how soon that pledge would be challenged.

Yosuke gave his blessing and Hideo went straight to the dress shop. He waited outside until Mitsue closed up and locked the door. When she looked at him she recognized his expression. She'd seen it before—four times before, to be exact. This time she said yes. They hugged and took the train home.

Mitsue was in no rush to marry. She thought that they could take the time during their year-long engagement to get to know each other better. That was the plan.

December 7, 1941, started out just like any other day. Mitsue woke up and ate a little porridge for breakfast. Her mother walked into the living room and switched on the CBC. The announcer spoke in a feverish tone. There had been a "Jap attack." Tomi fell to her knees.

CHAPTER 3

No Good

Fourteen months before Pearl Harbor, on September 15, 1940, Ralph MacLean left Grindstone as a rifleman. He had had two months of hurry-up-and-wait basic training in Valcartier, Quebec. The men wanted to get out into the world, they wanted to fight. They got to do neither. Their first international garrison duty was guarding

Gander's airport for nine monotonous months. The only action Ralph saw was guarding the officers' liquor chest.

Finally, the call came. The men were buzzing with anticipation. They were being reassigned. No one knew where they were going. They had no idea what their campaign had in store for them.

Before their next scheduled deployment, the men from the Magdalen Islands were granted a brief leave to return home. It had been months since Ralph had been with his family and he was keen to see them all, especially his mother. He knew she had been worried about him and that she would only be satisfied when she laid eyes on him and could see for herself that he was in good condition and well fed—even if it was not with her home cooking.

The night before they were to leave, Ralph's cousin Henry Clark took them on a caper. Ralph had never really liked his cousin. Henry was a troubled guy. He had a short fuse and was quick to violence. He reminded Ralph of his own father.

But Henry was his cousin, so when he stole a turkey from the Officers' Mess and needed a hand from Ralph to get it off the base, Ralph obliged. Family is family. The two of them snuck off the grounds and cooked the turkey at the home of an acquaintance of Henry's just a few blocks from the barracks. Later they stumbled home drunk and full to bursting, singing old Maritime songs. They were headed home to the island and glad of it.

But Ralph did not return to a happy home. His father had fallen ill with tuberculosis. Not that it made much difference to Ralph. He had left the island in large part because of his father's brutality. But he found his mother stricken with anxiety. He hated to see his mother in anguish. It left him puzzled—Stanley MacLean had been as cruel to her as he had to him. Why was she grieving? Ralph was not.

After a few more nights visiting friends and family and playing cards, it was almost time to go. Bur Ralph's mother had a going-away surprise for him. She did something she'd never done before: she threw a party. Nothing big, nothing fancy, just a small gathering of folks, some baking, some tea, and a few fiddles. Ralph's army pals were invited: Deighton, Bookie Leslie, Joe Delaney, and the Arsenault boys. His mother frowned on liquor, but Bookie saw to it that a flask was passed around discreetly.

The folks of Grindstone were proud of their boys. Not one of them over twenty-two, the boys puffed with pride as well. English and French floated through the house. As always, a fiddle was passed down the hall and into the living room, a couch was pushed aside, and a jig was born. They danced into the night, oblivious to what awaited them.

Ralph knew that there was one formality he needed to attend to. He had to see—and say goodbye to—his father. Stanley had been on bedrest the whole time Ralph was home, upstairs in the master bedroom. In his eighteen years, Ralph had rarely set foot in the room a mere two doors down from his. He had spent his whole life avoiding his father. As he entered the darkened room, he could hear his shallow breath. He was dying; that much was clear. Ralph stood above him. He did not touch him.

"Goodbye, Father."

That was that. If you can't say anything kind, don't say anything. He turned and closed the door behind him.

Ralph returned to base at Valcartier to find the regiment turning in their regular clothes for lightweight uniforms built for hot climates. They were getting inoculations. When Deighton saw Ralph, he pushed through the men waiting in line. "Word is we're going to the tropics, Ralph! The Winnipeg Grenadiers just came back from Jamaica and they need replacements! Jamaaaaica!"

Deighton was mad with excitement. The whole crew was. For most of these men, seeing the aqua blue waters of the Caribbean was a distant dream. For several generations, the families of these men had toiled on the land or on the sea, venturing only so far as the lobster would take them.

The very next morning, the men were told to pack their bags and return in an hour; they were departing by train to their next mission. In the barracks, the excitement was palpable. The men had sun, sand, and rum on their minds. Ralph was diligently folding his clothes when the platoon officer entered. All men stood at attention as Sergeant Tulk made his way down the centre aisle of the barrack hut. Tulk had a sincere composure to him. He had survived the poisonous trenches of the First World War. Most of his pals were dead, buried in unmarked graves scattered across western Europe. He slowly made his way to Ralph.

"Rifleman MacLean, come with me."

"Yes, sir," Ralph replied, his mind racing. He caught his cousin's eye as he followed his sergeant out of the barracks.

Shit. They know about the turkey, Ralph thought. He followed silently two paces behind Sergeant Tulk through the centre field towards the Officers' Mess.

"Take a seat, Ralph," Tulk said.

Ralph sat down.

"Like whisky? Have a sip, it's Protestant."

What the hell was this all about? It was 10 a.m.—why was he being offered a drink by his commanding officer? He did as he was told.

"Son, I have received some sad news from your family. Your mother wired us this morning to have you informed that your father passed away yesterday afternoon. I'm very sorry."

Ralph bowed his head, nodded, and fidgeted with the glass.

"Now listen, I've made some arrangements. The Bren carriers won't depart for another week. You can go home to pay your respects and be back in time to make it out with them. It has all been taken care of, okay? Stay here and take a moment—finish your drink."

Tulk got up. He thought that the conversation was over.

"Sir, before you leave, may I speak freely?" Ralph said.

The sergeant nodded.

"See, I was just home. I said my goodbye. Truth be told, there wasn't much respect to be paid anyway. I wish that was not the case, but it is. So if you don't mind, sir, I'd like to stay with the men. I'm appreciative for all you have done in making the arrangements, but I belong here. I don't want to hang back."

The sergeant nodded.

"Well, Ralph, that is entirely up to you."

With that, Tulk put his hand on Ralph's shoulder and left.

Ralph did not attend his father's funeral. He felt he was where he should be, where he needed to be. The men were his family and he did not want his father holding him down any further. He'd had quite enough of that.

As the train from Valcartier weaved its way farther west across the Canadian Shield, the men wondered just where they were going. Jamaica was beginning to seem out of the question. By the time they were in the middle of the vast prairie wheat fields, their best guess was Singapore.

Throughout Asia, the British Empire was in atrophy. When presented with a proposal to add a contingent of British forces to Hong Kong, Sir Winston Churchill studied the map. He knew Hong Kong was indefensible. After a long and imposing silence, he simply said: "This is no good."

But Canada was eager to prove itself. Australian and New Zealand troops were helping in North Africa. With the Hong Kong decision, hubris carried the day. Mackenzie King gathered his cabinet. They pledged two battalions. Churchill accepted the Canadian troops. Both parties agreed they'd provide moral support to the beleaguered islanders. Passing political opportunism swept military logic out the door. Nearly two thousand Canadian souls were committed to reinforce a garrison the British had already substantially depleted. In so doing, the fate of 819 men was sealed. They would never return home. The remaining 1,155 survivors would be forgiven if they sometimes felt they were the unlucky ones.

When they finally got off the train in Vancouver, the boys knew they were headed to Asia. On the deck of the New Zealand steamship *Awatea*, with Vancouver's harbour in the distance, the officer in charge finally addressed the troops. Standing beside Ralph, Deighton asked what almost every other man on that deck was asking himself: *where the hell is Hong Kong?*

But concerns about finding Hong Kong on their issued map were quickly forgotten when the dinner bell rang out. The New Zealand cooks served a mountain of mutton. This led to near mutiny before the *Awatea* left Canadian waters. As the men stood and threw their plates to the ground in disgust, Ralph stayed seated with his head down. He ate what was placed in front of him without complaint. He ate extra that night. This trait would serve him very, very well in the coming days.

The *Awatea* steamed into Pearl Harbor in Hawaii. The men hung off the edge of the boat, gawking at the beautiful, exotic women dancing the hula. They were itching to get off the boat and into some trouble, but were soundly refused. Instead, for the next hour Canadian bills rained off the side of the *Awatea* as Hawaiian women danced farewell. Ralph's hands stayed firmly in his pockets.

Ralph stayed on deck long after the women were out of sight. Later, as they steamed away from Pearl Harbor, he witnessed the most beautiful sunset he had ever seen. The sky and coast was awash in reds, pinks, and a golden yellow. It seemed as if the harbour had been set ablaze.

After nineteen days at sea, the *Awatea* arrived in Hong Kong Harbor. It was greeted by six decrepit planes and a few naval patrol boats. Unbeknownst to the men, the British had already evacuated their largest ships to Singapore. The *Awatea* sailed up to Holt's Wharf at Kowloon.

Kowloon is a city in mainland China, across the harbour from Victoria on the island of Hong Kong. It was then—and still is—referred to as the New Territories, and consists of a small crescent of land some twenty miles wide.

The men disembarked the *Awatea* like a bunch of tourists, not one of them with any sense of the place or of the danger they were in. They were intoxicated by the beautiful women and the tropical heat. They thought they had won the lottery, and anticipated nothing but good from their exotic destination.

The men were greeted on the wharf by the Governor of Hong

Kong and throngs of local inhabitants. Everyone was smiling and waving. Deighton and Ralph made formation and commenced the four-mile march down Nathan Road to the Shamshuipo barracks. Along the way, the exotic scents of the East enveloped the men, inviting them in. The warm, humid air put them at ease. The smiles gave them a false sense of security.

The progression down Nathan Road was a march unlike any the men had experienced. Everywhere they looked, they saw people. In every shop and restaurant, and down every little alleyway, there was someone doing something.

For the boys from the Magdalen Islands, the next three weeks would be the closest to royal treatment they would ever experience. They were billeted in the Shamshuipo barracks, which was right next to the dockyard. Constructed for the British troops in 1927, it had an air of empire to it. The grounds were orderly, with green grass growing in the well-maintained courtyard. Chinese boys scuttled to and fro as servants, helping the men with their gear, asking to clean their shoes, cook them some meat. Mosquito nets hung over every standard-issue and precisely made bed. The concrete floors were swept clean, the bedding neatly tucked in. Everything seemed in order.

Ralph found his assigned bunk, unloaded his gear, and walked the perimeter of the camp to get his bearings. The camp sat atop steep cliffs that looked out over the harbour. It was a beautiful, expansive view. The Chinese junks with their large painted sails, which ferried goods and people across the harbour, looked like they were from another time. From these peaks, he could see Hong Kong Island. It, too, seemed a bustling place. Ringing the north side of the camp was a long, winding road that hugged the coast. The road led to downtown Kowloon, where a group of men headed just as soon as their commanding officers let them.

Major MacAuley gathered all the men in the centre courtyard. The excited group stood at attention with the greatest of difficulty. They were, after all, just boys. Most had never ventured out of their province before enlisting. The foreign sights and smells outside the camp walls enticed their imagination. Now, halfway around the world, they were eager to soak up the sun and see what kind of fun they could find. The major reminded the boys of their obligation to their regiment and their country. No funny business.

Ralph and Deighton met up with a crew that had already grouped together by the camp's main gate. They left camp as quickly as the major's words left their minds. In Kowloon, they first hit an open market. Food was prepared on the street, and fine silks in every colour hung from the vendors' stalls.

"Ralphie, look at this place! Look at these prices! We're going to live like kings."

Deighton was right. The conversion rate was six Hong Kong dollars for every Canadian one. Even after the twenty-dollars-per-month that went to his mother, Ralph had about $130 Hong Kong dollars to spend on anything he wanted. It went a long way, and he came back from his first venture with some silk for baby Alayne. He also bought his mother a teapot; she was so fond of a good cup of tea. He told himself that he'd mail it as soon as he could. He would never get the chance.

By the time Ralph and Deighton made it back to camp, some soldiers had already hired local Chinese boys as personal servants to shave them, shine their shoes, and wash and press their clothes. Some men really lived it up from day one. The company's shoemaker lost no time and promptly moved off base with a Chinese woman. Ralph could not let himself part with his money so easily. He would shave himself, thank you very much. He was determined not to get too carried away in this new world.

The first night ended with a big feast put on by many of the local folks to welcome their new Canadian guardians. There was beef, rice, shrimp dumplings, green tea, and, of course, a good amount of beer. Ralph went to bed with a full belly and a smile on his face. Things were looking up for him and his pals. This was going to be a breeze. For the next three weeks the men spent their days lazily preparing the camp and their nights taking the rickshaws into town to hit the SunSun Café. They fraternized with the locals, playing ball with the local Portuguese ball team and getting into the odd brawl with their British comrades. The only enemy was the daily hangover.

Nothing lasts forever. Not with fifty thousand hardened Japanese troops coming at you with all their might.

December 7, 1941, started out like any other day for Ralph in his new home. But as he was finishing eggs and coffee for breakfast, he saw Deighton rush into the mess hall, eyes ablaze.

"Ralphie! Judas!"

Deighton grabbed Ralph by the arm. "Get under your gear! The Japs are coming hard at us. They hit everywheres: Hawaii, Guam . . . you name it. The major thinks we got over fifty thousand of 'em coming straight for us."

PART 2

The War Years

Chapter 4

Pearl Harbor

Ralph quickly did the math. He knew they only had fourteen thousand men. He was a signalman, and he knew that the company's heavy weapons would not land for another week. They were mistakenly sent to the Philippines.

Outnumbered nearly four to one and with no air force or navy, the Hong Kong garrison was doomed. Ralph thought of his father. If he had gone to the funeral, he would most certainly have been on the boats now en route to the Philippines. Maybe his father would get the last laugh after all.

It was decided that a small group would stay on the mainland and set up a security line just outside Kowloon. The Gin Drinker's Line would be the first line of defence. The Scots and the Indians would defend the ten-mile line just north of Kowloon with enough men to hold out for as long as they could. The Royal Rifles would defend the east under Brigadier Cedric Wallis and the Winnipeg Grenadiers would defend the west under Major Christopher Maltby—the overall commander—would base his operation out of the Peninsula Hotel.

Ralph boarded a small boat with Bookie, Leslie, and Deighton and crossed the harbour. It took all afternoon. Setting foot for the first time on the island they were charged with defending, they congregated at Aldrich Bay. An officer addressed the men. He got them cheering.

Ralph was in Headquarters Company, a group of specialists: carpenters, signalmen, cooks, and drivers. They were, by necessity, spread out as needed across the western part of the island. The problem was that nobody really knew what was needed. Confusion reigned and the Canadians scrambled to prepare for an attack. Ralph spotted his commanding officer, Lieutenant Peter MacDougall, a half-mile down the road. Half the company surrounded him. Ralph dashed over and tugged on Bookie's sleeve.

"Where is everyone else?" Ralph asked.

"Who the hell knows? I hear a bunch of our guys got stranded back at Shamshuipo."

"Ralph, come up here," the CO called. He was opening a large map of the surrounding area. "We don't know where the Japs are going to land. Take these three men and head to this town—" He pointed at Sheko. "I don't have any trucks for you, so you better be off at first light tomorrow."

Ralph nodded. The CO put his hand on his shoulder. "Rifleman, if you see troops landing, shoot to kill. If you see any light at night, shoot it to hell."

Ralph nodded again. His mouth was so dry he could barely muster "Yes, sir."

"Good luck. I'll send a runner up for you with some food and water."

That was it. With a slap on the back, Ralph had entered the war.

The men slept on the side of the road that night. Most had trouble getting to sleep in the open air. None of them knew this would be the most sleep they'd get for the next fourteen days.

At dawn, Ralph awoke. He took a deep breath as the previous day's events washed over him. Bookie was up and making a little coffee with an army-issue pot and a small grass-fed fire. He waved Ralph over.

"Be right there. Gotta make some water." Ralph said as he made his way to the road's edge away from the guys. He had a view of the harbour and the clear dawn sky. With wispy clouds blowing in from the open ocean, it didn't look that much different from the sky back home. He wondered if his mother had heard about the attacks of the day before. He started to do his business, looking down as he peed on the dark green grass. When he looked back up, he saw three dark specks falling hard out of the clouds. He zipped and ran.

Minutes later the sky was full of buzzing Japanese Zero airplanes, a nest of hornets swooping in and out of the ocean-blown clouds. They were strafing Shamshuipo and the Gin Drinker's line. Ralph stood with the other men. A grave silence befell them. All they could do was watch and listen to the horrific first sounds of war, a wave of explosions that struck fear into their souls. This fear was to become their constant companion.

Ralph looked at his watch: 6 a.m. Time to move. He and his companions set out for Sheko, a town he'd never heard of on an island he only knew by the lines of the map he held in his hand. They caught a ride for part of the journey and then walked south for fifteen hours straight.

Sheko was not so much a town as a few houses on the southern cliffs of Hong Kong. By the end of the day, the four men had traversed the entire island. They had not stopped once. Their feet were on fire with blisters the likes of which they've never felt before. The final three hours they had had to cut their way through heavy brush as the road had been washed out. One of the chaps had had the foresight to bring a machete. Without it, they might never have reached their objective.

For the next five days, these men experienced the war in slow-motion. They saw nothing of the fighting. They heard only the loudest of explosions off in the distance, like the thunder claps that rang off the cliffs of Pleasant Bay. This was the army's standard of hurry-up-and-wait at its most agonizing.

The angels were smiling on Ralph and the other three men during those 120 hours. In that time, the Gin Drinker's Line had been completely overrun. It took the Japanese only two hours. The men who survived the heavy aerial assault and fierce ground attacks were pulled back onto the island. With the mainland completely in their control, the Japanese army set up their heavy artillery and began to shell the island. The Canadians could only take cover and wait for the impending ground assault.

The bombing was intense throughout the day. The thunderous roar sounded like hell had opened up on the north side of the island. Ralph took the watch as the other men caught a bit of sleep.

The Japanese artillery pounded the island. They were systematically blasting away at all the fortified positions along the coastline, one after another. It seemed to the Canadians that they were waiting in line for their destruction. When they would take up a new position, the artillery would find them with unfailing accuracy. Artillery shells fell like rain. Everything within range was left in rubble. Troops' movements were pinpointed and targeted. It took the defenders two days to realize that their communication system had been compromised.

Ralph and the three men with him were cut off. They had no idea what was happening except that their friends were taking a heavy beating. The sound of falling bombs had them all on edge. Sammy Shane, an American with a Thompson submachine gun, was the jumpiest. He heard a twig snap and unloaded his entire clip into a bush. The culprit, a small brown rabbit, escaped unscathed.

At dusk, after a shared can of bully beef, Ralph took watch again. The others tried to catch a few moments of sleep. They were atop a small hill overlooking a few houses and the shoreline. The wind had begun to pick up, blowing in low-lying clouds, ensuring a dark night without stars. Ralph had just given one of the guys lying beside him a little shove to keep him from snoring. Sitting on his cot, wrapped in his blanket, he saw a flash of light. Or at least he thought he did. Your mind plays tricks on you after days of fear and nothingness. He grabbed his rifle and chambered a round with the bolt action. Standing, he raised and pointed the rifle in the direction of that flicker of light. He had yet to fire a gun in anger. He heard the CO's voice running through his mind: *if you see a light, shoot it to hell.*

There it was, the same light. It looked to be coming from one of the houses of Sheko. It was impossible to tell for sure. The light went off and on twice. Was it a message? Again, impossible to tell. Nor did it matter: Ralph had his orders. He lined the light up in his sights and squeezed the trigger, then chambered another round and fired again. The three sleeping lads leaped out of their blankets. They were standing beside him with their rifles drawn by the time he chambered a third round.

"A light, just to our three o'clock," Ralph whispered.

The light flickered again.

All four men opened up. They heard one bullet ricochet off something tin or metal. The light went out. It did not come back on.

Ralph's shift was up. He had taken no pleasure in his first piece of action. He unrolled his blanket and tried his best to fall asleep.

He awoke to the sound of heavy footsteps. It was a runner sent from headquarters. He came with water and another few cans of bully beef.

"How are you guys doing? See anything?" he asked.

"Shot at a few lights last night. Other than that, nothing," Ralph reported.

"Well, consider yourselves lucky. We are taking a beating on the north end. The shells just won't stop. They've already taken half our pillboxes out along the coast. It's only a matter of time before they're all gone. We'll only have the forest as cover by the time the Japs land," the runner predicted.

"Any other news?" one of the guys asked.

"A good hundred guys are dead. Bodies are washing up every-where. Wish I had better news for you. I gotta get back. Take care, guys." And with that, the runner disappeared into the thick brush along the path that Ralph had cut a few days before.

The following three days brought the same constant drone of artillery explosions in the distance. And then the same runner, looking liked he'd aged a decade, popped out from the bush. He was the first human being Ralph and the others had seen in six days.

The runner led them to Palm Villa, which had been a vacation resort before the war. Now Japanese forces were everywhere. The runner waved his arm and they all crouched down behind some thick brush, then he pulled a pair of binoculars from his pack and found an opening in the shrubs. He searched back and forth, up and down.

"Okay, looks like it hasn't been overrun yet. Let's go."

Yet? Ralph thought as he followed, crouching as low as he could. As they ran alongside the edge of the once-manicured garden, Ralph took in the level of devastation. The building, a turn-of-the-century seaside luxury retreat, had been heavily shelled. Bullet holes riddled the front door and most of the windows had been shot out. The runner hit the side door and it opened to a scene of total chaos. Ralph saw Major MacAuley, his arm bloodied and heavily bandaged, screaming into a phone in order to be heard over the explosions at the other end of the line. A report of relative calm came in from the northwest sector, immediately followed by a report that the northwest sector was being overrun.

"I need five men to head down to the road. I can't find our goddamn Bren carrier!" the CO said. The Bren gun carrier was one of the few to have made it to the island. The truck was crucial for moving the only heavy guns the Canadians had. Without it, they had only their .303 Lee-Enfield rifles.

Everybody knew how important this mission was. Twenty men stood up immediately. The CO counted them off: you, you, you, you, and you. The five chosen dashed out the door that Ralph just entered. Within minutes, they were all back, with one drunken addition.

"The Bren gun carrier is smashed to hell 150 yards down the road, sir," a man reported. The scent of whisky filled the lobby.

The CO became enraged; he knew the driver was drunk. Throwing down the map he'd been poring over, he took the driver by the collar and punched him in the face three times, then threw him to the floor. Standing over him, he demanded, "Do you know what you've done?"

It was only a matter of time now. Everyone in the room knew it, even the drunken driver. The poor chap had been trying to dull his sense of the inevitable.

Ralph found a corner in one of the bedrooms. He had not slept in three straight days. The tile floor felt cool on his face. His reprieve was momentary. Joe Delaney woke him up.

"Ralph, I thought that was you. Come on, I need some help. We gotta get some ammo up to the boys on Mount Parker. A group of ten of us are going."

Ralph rubbed his eyes. He hadn't seen Joe since the invasion and was glad to know he was still alive.

"Where's Mount Parker?" Ralph asked.

"A few miles up from here. Let's go," Joe said as he popped up from his crouched position.

"Okay," Ralph groaned, desperately longing for more sleep. As they made their way down the hall, stepping over men, some wounded, some sleeping, some shell-shocked, Ralph grabbed Joe's arm. Joe turned. They looked at each other's dirty faces and red, sleep-deprived eyes. Ralph smiled.

"Joe, we are a hell of a long way from our Grindstone."

Neither had thought of home for some time. Joe chuckled.

"That we are. That we are."

They made their way through the mess hall into the storage area in the back of the Villa. An old closet that had been used to store pineapples and mangoes was now stacked to the roof with boxes of .303 shells and some grenades. The men loaded the bandoliers over their shoulders.

"Take as much as you can carry. The guys on Parker are getting the shit kicked outta them," hollered the guard.

Ralph was loaded up like a pack mule. The metal shells dug into his sweat-drenched fatigues. He heaved forward to support them against his neck and hugged his sides to keep them from swaying as he ran to catch up with the other nine. The ten men stood five to a side, hugging the narrow hallway to the back door. They knelt down. The sentry at the door looked them over and explained.

"We had a sniper out here a few hours ago. I think we took him out, but we've been suppressing fire every time this door opens. When I give you the go-ahead, hit the door hard; take the trail at your four o'clock into the bush. Run, you hear? Do not look back and do not stop."

The sentry stood up and wiped his forehead. "Give me a minute, I'll give the gunner a thirty-second warning."

The men waited. Joe was behind Ralph. He put his hand on Ralph's shoulder.

"Thanks for that, Ralph. I hadn't thought of home in some time."

Ralph nodded, and then they heard the sentry's call.

"Go, men, go!"

The first man hit the door with his shoulder and the rest followed under the roar of a Bren gun.

The men marched the trail in two lines of five. The heat of the jungle quickly wore them down. Two miles in, the point stopped, knelt down on one knee, and held his arm in a fist. The other nine did the same. They all paused, listening for anything. For everything. The point jumped off the trail into the deep bush. Again, the men followed suit. Ralph landed right beside Joe, both men gripping their rifles, pointed for action.

Footsteps.

Ralph peered through the bush to see if it was friend or foe. The weary shuffling gave them away: they were Canadians. Ralph sighed and stood up to see a column of men, most barely able to walk, coming down the trail.

The other party's scout approached Ralph's lead man. The other nine just stood and stared as the defeated-looking soldiers walked by. The men did not look up as they passed.

Ralph and the nine others all approached their leader, though they needed no explanation of what had just transpired.

"That's all that's left of Mount Parker," the leader said.

"At least we won't have to hump all this ammo up that hill," one of the guys said, as they all turned and marched back to Palm Villa.

When they returned, an officer ran through the line, grabbing men at random for another short mission. Ammo was needed to the south of Palm Villa. Joe went. He never came back. When Ralph returned later that day, he saw a long line of bodies under blankets. He wondered if Joe was under one of them, but he was too exhausted to shed a tear.

It was seventeen days since the attack on Pearl Harbor. The men who were still alive were too tired to care. They were straggling in, two and three at a time, to the relative safety of Palm Villa. Many had spent the previous few days lost, wandering the hills without food or water. Most had not slept a wink. Everyone had watched a pal, a cousin, or a brother die.

Sniper fire was everywhere and the men were no longer able to exit the site without a hail of suppressing fire. A simple fact became increasingly clear: Palm Villa was a death trap.

The men tried to keep their spirits up. They clung to rumours of rescue like life rafts. *The Chinese guerrillas may launch a counterattack from the north. The Brits have sent rescue ships from Singapore.* They were lies told by men desperate for hope to equally desperate men.

On his second day at Palm Villa, Ralph resumed his position as a signalman. He was stationed in the operations room, where the officers were sending orders and receiving news from the few soldiers that had communication capabilities. None of the news was good. It was death across the island.

Of the four Canadian companies, only D Company remained largely intact, stationed around Chung Hom Kok. This would not last. Company A had been cut off in and around Repulse Bay. They paid dearly for their isolation, losing over half their men. Company B was scattered throughout the island's high ground around Mount Stanley. Companies C and H.Q. were huddled in Palm Villa. Everyone knew they had only a few hours left there. Japanese heavy artillery was pounding all held positions. Japanese airplanes owned the sky, swooping in and strafing the men whenever and wherever they were forced into a clearing. Japanese navy supply ships sat off the coast, loaded with food, ammunition, and supplies. Almost every man could see the sea from where he stood and fought. The sea was the last line. There would be no retreat from the shore.

Ralph sat at his assigned wooden table, receiver in hand. Each incoming report had to be shouted over heavy gunfire. Men, good men, men Ralph knew well, were dying. Dairy farmers from Sherbrooke, seamen from Cape Breton, woodsmen from Bathurst. Few were older than twenty. They'd been shot up in a strange land by an unknown enemy.

Ralph grew increasingly frustrated with each incoming message he passed on. He kept thinking one thought over and over: *this is not a fair fight*. His pals didn't stand a chance out there. They knew it, the officers knew it, and *their* officers knew it. Churchill was right: the defence of Hong Kong was no good. And it was about to get a whole lot worse.

"We're taking heavy fire in the Stanley sector!" a Scotsman screamed over the radio. The officers got quiet. They knew that if they lost Stanley Fort, it would all be over. There would be nowhere to go but the sea.

"We can't lose Stanley. We lose it, we are done for. Grab as many able men as you can find. We have to make sure that the Japs don't set up their heavy mortars to shell Stanley. We'll leave at twenty-two-hundred hours," Officer MacDougall ordered.

Ralph did as he was told. Armed with the reports he had been ferrying for the past few hours, he purposely chose no one he knew to come on the mission. He felt it was suicidal. Nonetheless, at twenty-two-hundred hours, he and twelve other men joined the captain at the back door of the Villa. Between them they had two canisters of water, three cans of bully beef, one Bren gun with three bandoliers of shells, five hand grenades, and enough .303 shells to last one—maybe two—real firefights.

Ralph said a prayer. He asked God to watch over him. He asked for mercy. He sought grace. Ralph had never had to make this call before. As he had three days earlier, he found himself crouched in a line of men, single file, at the back door of Palm Villa. They gripped their rifles and waited for their call to move.

"Suppressing fire!"

The ring of discharged shells rattled down the hallway.

"Move!" the sentry bellowed.

The point man made a cross against his chest, kissed his fingers, and hit the door with his shoulder. The men dashed into the bush and regrouped five hundred yards from the Villa at the rally point. They counted off and, all accounted for, began their trek through a deep valley. Darkness was their ally and their enemy. It hid them from the enemy but made it all but impossible to see their way through the dense brush. The men took turns carrying the heavy Bren gun. The persistent buzz of Japanese planes ensured the guy with the Bren gun kept one eye to the sky.

The men clutched their rifles as they trudged through the night. Every broken branch they heard brought them to a standstill, wary. They made their way down a steep hill, grasping at branches and roots as they slipped their way down. Midway down, Ralph saw three shadows. He squinted. The long bayonets were the telltale sign. He raised his rifle and squeezed the trigger again and again. He didn't think, he just shot, just as he had been trained. He had his sights on the last man and saw the silhouette go down. Was he shot or had he jumped into a water catchment? There was no way to know. Ralph may have killed a man, he may have not. The threat gone, he continued down the steep embankment.

At the edge of the valley, the CO stopped the men and called for Ralph. Ralph hustled up. The CO pulled a blanket over his head and shone his flashlight at the map. As Ralph ducked in, the light momentarily blinded him. The two men pored over the map, running their dirty fingers along the line representing the trail they were on.

"We'll cross this creek, proceed through this clearing, and dig in on this hill. From there, we'll fight like hell to keep the Japs from setting up and shelling the village and Stanley Fort," the CO decided out loud.

"Yes, sir."

"How are the men, Ralph?" the CO asked as their bloodshot eyes met.

"They are scared. But they are holding up, sir," Ralph responded.

"*Volens et valens.*" The CO gave Ralph a wink and a smile.

"*Volens et valens,*" Ralph repeated. A show of bravado is sometimes the best medicine.

On his way back down to the line to assume his position among the men, Ralph swapped out and took Bren gun duty.

Dawn was breaking on Christmas Day. The men waded through a little creek at full attention. If spotted, they were sitting ducks. They tried to make as little sound as possible with each step. One by one, they made it to the water's edge and waited, guns pointed, searching for movement in the deep brush. Large explosions were heard in the background. The daily dawn assault was underway. It had become part of their routine. It could be counted on more than breakfast.

Once across the creek, the men crouched in the tall grass. The CO gave them a brief reprieve to wring out their socks and share what meagre food they had. Ralph pulled out the spoon that was in his shirt pocket, rinsed it off in the creek, and got in on an open can of bully beef that two other men were already sharing. Somewhere down the line, one man quietly hummed "Silent Night."

With damp socks donned again, the men gathered their gear and peeked out of the grass. The clearing they needed to cross was a full mile. A point man went out first. The rest of the men waited in silence but heard no gunfire. The CO waved them on, each man saying a little prayer as he stepped out from the cover of the brush. The dawn sun was already warm and Ralph was thinking about how the men were going to need more water than they had to last the day. He was thinking maybe they should have bottled some of that creek water, when he heard an unmistakable sound. He looked up at the men. They were continuing on course, their eyes on the trees on the other side of the clearing. Maybe his mind was playing tricks on him. Instinctively, he gripped the Bren gun a little tighter. No, there it was again. Ralph took a knee and scanned the sky. The sun was bright. He squinted hard. If he was right, he had only a few seconds more to act. And there it was, getting louder and closing in, the incendiary Zero. Its green-tipped wings with the red Rising Sun were the last thing many Canadian men saw before dying.

"Plane!" Ralph yelled.

The whole squad hit the ground, each man on his belly, eyes frantically searching the sky. They were smack dab in the middle of the clearing, too far out to run back to the grass, too far from the treeline to make a dash for it.

"Hold, men," the CO warned.

One man could not contain his fear and jumped up and tried to run. Another tackled him immediately.

"Stay the hell down!" someone else yelled.

Their only hope was that the pilot of the lone plane would not spot them. Ralph loaded the Bren gun and readied himself. He looked at his watch. It was 6:32 a.m. Back home, his mother would be cleaning up from Christmas dinner.

The plane did one loop high above the clearing. Maybe they were in the clear. Ralph could hear one man whispering to himself, "Just go . . . just go." The plane's engines accelerated and it began to descend. It was bearing down on them. The CO screamed a life or death order: "Ralph, keep him off!"

Ralph scrambled off his belly, braced his knee into the dirt, and hoisted the Bren into position. The plane opened up on them and a hail of bullets tore into the ground. Ralph took dead aim at the plane, drew a deep breath, and squeezed the trigger. The gun released a burst of angry little angels into the sky. Ralph fired until he ran out of bullets. Fourteen lives depended on him and that Bren gun.

Through his scope, he saw the plane bank to the right. The pilot was veering away from the clearing, away from them.

"Move! Move! Move!" screamed the CO.

All the men heard the terror in his voice.

Ralph grabbed the ammo, threw it over his shoulder, and ran as fast as he could. He was the last to hit the treeline. He collapsed beside two men, both scanning the sky.

"I think it's gone," Ralph said, too tired to join the two others in their search. He leaned against a tree, head back, mouth open.

The CO crawled over to them.

"Have a drink of water, Ralph. That was some fine firing. You gave it to that S.O.B.," he said as he unscrewed his water canteen and passed it over.

"I thought he had our number," one of the guys nearby stated matter-of-factly.

"Okay, men, we can't wait here for that pilot to radio in our location. Let's move out."

The group trudged up the hill overlooking Stanley Fort. They could have sworn the mud had hands that pulled their boots in deeper. They could see the fort and the surrounding village through the breaks in the forest. Steep hills ringed it on all sides; the sunlight glistened off the sea. From their vantage point, they could see several unattended fires raging. The men set up a perimeter defence, which consisted of seven men forming a small semicircle around the remaining seven, spaced a few paces apart. They had begun digging their own foxholes when three shots rang out. Everyone hit the ground.

The three men on the left flank returned fire. Ralph saw two Japanese soldiers run down the hill. They had light, mustard green fatigues and hats with tails. Their rifles were long and each had a bayonet attached. The men were short and had black hair. They were the first Japanese soldiers Ralph had ever seen. Fortunately, they were going the other way, running back to the new base of Japanese operations: Palm Villa.

"I can't get any response from the base. The line is just dead, Captain," the radioman reported.

Ralph was sharing a can of corned beef with two other guys. As he leaned over to take his next turn at the tin, the man holding it was hit twice in the chest. The bullets landed with a *thwap*, burying themselves into his lungs and ribs. He slumped over and the tin rolled out of his hands. Time stood still for a brief moment as bullets came from all sides. They were caught in their enemy's crosshairs. There was nowhere to go. Ralph scanned his left. He could see three men firing their single-action rifles as fast as they could. To his right, one man was staggering aimlessly, screaming, his stomach completely opened up. Ralph shot his rifle in the direction of some of the incoming fire. Two grenade explosions shook the ground behind Ralph's position. He could hear the cries of several men.

"Every man for himself!" MacDougall cried.

Ralph saw a small cliff about fifteen yards down the hill. He grabbed the guy beside him by the collar.

"There! There!" he pointed. "Let's tuck in down there!" he screamed over the gunfire that was hitting the leaves like a metal rain.

Ralph crouched down, leading the way, picking up two other men as he ran. The bullets cut into the branches and exploded above their heads. Another grenade detonated, propelling the fourth man into a tree. His mangled body wrapped around the trunk. The bullets were missing Ralph by inches, each buzzing by with a zing as it cut through the air, hungry for flesh.

The three men reached the cliff and leaped over, not even knowing what was on the other side. Away from the bullets was destination enough. They landed on a ledge six feet below. Ralph fell hard on his side. The wind was knocked out of him and his rifle flew out of his hands. He watched it tumble down the steep hill. The force of the fall broke the leg of the second man on the ledge. They looked for the third man in vain.

Neither man had a rifle. Ralph instinctively drew his knife. Fifteen yards above him were at least thirty Japanese soldiers with machine guns. The second man was crouched down in near hysterics as heavy machinegun fire rang out unabated. The two did not hear any further .303 gunshots in response. Anyone left alive was hiding, crouched somewhere, hoping that they were not experiencing their final moments. They could hear a few of their buddies groaning and weeping, imagining this was the end.

The sun was steaming hot and Ralph swallowed hard. Between his fear and the heat, there was no moisture in his mouth at all. He knelt down, back firmly against the hill, to pat his comrade's back. He did not have the gall to say everything would be all right. The view from the ledge was beautiful and Ralph was struck again by a sense of irony.

Suddenly Ralph laughed. He laughed and looked down at the man hunched beside him.

"Merry Christmas," he said.

CHAPTER 5

Celtic, British Columbia

It felt as if the bombs of Pearl Harbor had been dropped on Mitsue's living room.

The family had the radio tuned to the CBC. They were trying to get as much information as they could. As the devastation revealed itself, Yosuke stood up from the kitchen table, slowly walked through to the living room, and clicked off the radio. He turned and everyone stared into his weary eyes.

They had never before prayed as a family. But that afternoon, for the first time, they sat in a circle on the living room floor. Susanne was the first to ask the question that everyone in the house, and every Japanese Canadian in British Columbia, was thinking: "What will happen to us now?"

Yosuke knew that this crisis would be used by people who wanted the Japanese fishermen out of the industry to whip up fear and drive them away from the coast, away from the fish. He knew right away what was coming. And he knew that it would come wrapped in the Canadian flag in the name of national security. He knew that the only thing the government wanted to secure was the fishing stocks.

By midafternoon, reports of arrests were trickling out of Little Tokyo. Everyone was on edge. That night they went to bed afraid of what tomorrow's newspaper headline would be.

And sure enough, the very next day the headline confirmed their worst fears: CANADA AT WAR, JAPS FORCED OUT. Yosuke went down to the dockyard where both his boats were moored and he saw police and some of his friends standing around. It had begun. Every single boat owned by a Japanese fisherman, Canadian or not, had been seized. There could be no more fishing. The boats were to be taken away and locked up. Over one thousand of them would be tied up and left to sit idle. By the end of the day, the seized boats stretched out along the Fraser River made it difficult to see the water.

Yosuke was crushed. For so long he had tried to make sure that something like this would not happen. But world events had undermined him. There was nothing he could do. He wasn't even allowed to board his boats to retrieve the books he had left there, including his Bible. The RCMP ordered him to leave immediately. He complied.

Some of the men cried as they left the dock. Yosuke tried to comfort a few of them. They were inconsolable. One man cried out, "How will I feed my children?" Yosuke didn't have the answer to that. He wondered the same thing. The effect of that afternoon was devastating: over eighteen hundred men with families depending on them, all out of work. The round-up took three hours.

Yosuke returned home and tried to conceal his concern. He just said: "They took our boats, we'll have to figure it out." He was trying to keep his wife and children positive. But he knew things would not get better. A few days later the RCMP came to Celtic and locked up the community centre. They knew exactly what they were doing. It was a school, a church, and a meeting place. The point was made.

For the next few weeks, rumours swirled everywhere around Mitsue—at home in Celtic, at the dress shop in Granville, and on Powell Street. She avoided Powell Street as much as she could. Everyone was so scared you could see it in their eyes. Everybody was worried about their families, their businesses, and their homes, but mostly their children. What was going to happen to them? Some thought everyone would be rounded up and sent back to Japan. Their world was getting smaller—closing in on them.

Mitsue felt a little safer than most. She was a Canadian citizen, after all. They wouldn't do all the terrible things people were talking about to Canadian citizens. She had been born here, all her brothers and sisters had been born here. She'd never even been to Japan. Canada was all she knew. She felt Canadian through and through. And even though she was not permitted to vote, Canada was a democracy. That meant it was a safe country. That is what she had learned in school, and she believed it.

The next two months shattered those beliefs. Fear and greed can do terrible things to the human heart. Every morning brought a fresh round of stories about windows on Powell Street being smashed in. People would just hurl rocks, bricks, or anything else they could find at Japanese storefronts. The insurance companies began to cancel the policies of Japanese owners. Everyone felt that same isolating feeling: there was nowhere to turn. So few were willing to help. Things were getting uglier by the day.

Mitsue kept going to work at the dress shop, praying each morning as she turned the corner that she would not find it burned or smashed. One morning just before Christmas, a woman who owned a dressmaking shop on Powell Street found a "black hand" note taped to her door. This had become common. The writers of these notes threatened to burn the places down if they didn't close. Mrs. Yamamoto had enough to worry about already. The shop was not on Powell Street, so a lot of her customers were white and many of them had stopped coming around. Her store had never been quiet at this time of the year. People were always buying dresses or having dresses mended before Christmas, but this year they weren't coming by the shop.

On Christmas Eve, Mitsue had a turkey dinner at home. The entire family was there: Yosuke and Tomi, Pat, Mary, and Susanne. Hideo came too. He and Mitsue had been engaged for just over a month. After they finished cleaning up, they were listening to the radio in the living room when a news flash came on. Mitsue hated the sound of the news flash—nothing good ever came from it.

Hong Kong had fallen. Over one thousand Canadian troops were now in Japanese hands. For the second time, the family prayed together. They prayed for the prisoners. They prayed for themselves.

Yosuke knew this was more bad news for his family. He was staring straight up at the tsunami that he had tried to avoid all those years ago when he had left Japan. It was about to wash away everything he had worked so hard for. He knew that it was only a matter of time until that wave crested right at his door.

The December 7 attack had left Ottawa reeling. The Japanese military machine had crippled the U.S. western fleet and its troops had moved swiftly and simultaneously through Malaysia, Guam, the

Philippines, and Wake Island. Their attack on the British fleet had left Hong Kong a sitting duck. Leaders in Canada were scrambling to bolster defences along the long western shoreline.

Anti-Japanese politicians saw this as their golden opportunity. They loaded their propaganda ammunition and opened fire. They bombarded the national press and charged at Prime Minister Mackenzie King with all they could muster. The anti-Japanese politicians from British Columbia had been held at bay for far too long; on December 17, 1941, they formed the Pacific Coast Security League. This league's sole purpose was to deport or remove all Japanese from British Columbia.

The first official proceeding took place in Ottawa on January 8 and 9, 1942. A parliamentary committee requested representatives from B.C.—many of whom had just founded the Security League— to meet with senior members of External Affairs, the RCMP, and the military. The fate of every Japanese-Canadian soul hung in the balance as these leaders met in a room in the basement of the nation's Parliament buildings. The men all held their positions as firmly as they gripped their dossiers.

The army made the first presentation. Major-General Maurice Pope, vice-chair of general staff of the Canadian Army, sat squarely in his chair and stated that the Canadian Armed Forces had no interest in the proposed evacuation. Even at the pinnacle of Japan's military prowess, the position of the Canadian military brass was that there was absolutely no need to consider moving the Japanese population from the coast. RCMP officials agreed with the army's assessment.

H.E. Reid, vice-admiral of the Navy, was up next. He reminded the committee members that all Japanese-owned vessels had been seized and confirmed that a naval threat was nonexistent.

Next, the B.C. politicians took the floor. They were led by George Pearson, B.C.'s minister of labour. He was half mad with rage. His position was that the entire Japanese population could not be trusted and he sought a final solution for his province: drive them all out. The committee chair, Ian Mackenzie, himself a B.C.

politician long known to harbour vehement anti-Japanese views, thanked Mr. Pearson and adjourned for the day.

Escott Reid, a long-time External Affairs official, later wrote, "I felt in that committee room in the presence of evil." Pearl Harbor was a gift to biggots who wanted to remove the Japanese from B.C. and its economy. It mattered little that Canada's national security—army, navy, and RCMP—were all on record stating there was no national security issue. Vitriol of that degree gets attention. It whips up, it grows, and it often wins.

Prime Minister Mackenzie King, ever the cautious politician, sought a compromise. On January 14 he announced that all Japanese aliens would be evacuated to protected areas that fell outside of a one-hundred-mile radius of the coast. It seemed King was hoping to avert the calls for a full Japanese evacuation by sacrificing those Japanese who had not yet become Canadian citizens. He failed.

As resentment hit the street, the Security League continued to incite intolerance among the general population. The prime minister was fearful of more race riots—the sort of violence that would make the riots of 1907 look like schoolyard tussles. King was also afraid that news of attacks on Japanese living in Canada would elicit harsh retribution against the Canadian soldiers being held in Hong Kong. He tried to solve the problem by sending the Japanese away. He banished them instead of protecting them.

After the call went out to evacuate those Japanese who weren't Canadian citizens, the fear was that all Japanese would be sent back to Japan, even those born in Canada. Lots of politicians were calling for this. Now that the Japanese boats had been confiscated, nothing seemed off-limits. Japanese Canadians had run out of high ground. There was no shelter to be had.

The one thing that was clear was that single men would be treated differently. They were being sent to work on road camps out east, where conditions were terrible. They felt like slaves.

Yosuke gathered his family into the living room for what he knew would be a critical family meeting.

Hideo and Mitsue decided to move up their wedding date. Not sure how long they had, they hastily set a date. This left Mitsue with a lot of work to do. She had to make a dress, find a place to get married, and plan a little party for their friends and family. She only had two weeks—perhaps not even that.

She spent the next fourteen days sewing her wedding dress and

the bridesmaids' dresses. Tomi had purchased Mitsue's wedding kimono three years earlier from family in Japan. It had chrysanthemums on the shoulders and all down the front and a beautiful white and pink obi that went around her waist. Mitsue would pin a flower in the back of her hair.

Mitsue sewed a traditional dress for the reception. It was a long silk dress with full sleeves. The sheer, train-length veil had scalloped edges and silk embroidered irises at each corner. Mrs. Yamamoto had helped her select the fabric. Mitsue was thankful for that. She and Hideo were getting married so quickly they hadn't had any time to save money. With the boats gone, everyone was trying to save the little cash they had. Nobody knew what was around the corner. On the fourteenth day, Mitsue finished her sister Mary's dress. Mary was to be her maid of honour.

Hideo and Mitsue were married on January 29, 1941, a cold and miserable day. Mitsue spent the morning getting ready at home in Celtic. It would be her last day there, as she would move to the boarding house with Hideo the next day. She liked her house better, but a wife had to live where her husband lived, not the other way around. Mary, Susanne, and her mother all helped her prepare.

At ten in the morning, Yosuke honked the horn from the driveway. Mitsue dashed outside and climbed into the car so as not to get her dress wet. She caught sight of Ichuri standing on the sidewalk, soaked to the bone. Tears ran down his face. He must have been standing in the cold, hard rain all morning.

Mitsue got out and went to him. "What are you doing?" she asked. He was shivering and crying. He begged her not to get married. He professed his love.

She felt so bad for him that she forgot about her dress, hair, and makeup. She put her hand on his forearm and pleaded with him to go home. It took some time, but he finally relented.

Mitsue got into the car and they made their way down to the church. Because of wartime rules restricting Japanese people from meeting in large numbers, Hideo and Mitsue had had to go to City Hall to get a permit for the fifty-five wedding guests.

When Mitsue and her family got to the church, they all walked up the stairs together. There were two RCMP guards at the front door to check the registration cards of all the guests. They wore uniforms and caps, and held clubs and guns. They demanded to see the family's registration cards. Everyone showed their card except Mitsue. She didn't have her registration card on her. There are no pockets in kimonos, and she wasn't carrying a purse.

"Where's yours?" the guard said, sticking his chin out. There was disrespect in his manner. Mary rooted around in her purse for her sister's registration card. The officer stared at Mitsue, who was worried that Mary had forgotten the card and they'd have to go all the way back to Celtic. Mary finally found the card and handed it to the officer. He took it and looked at it, looked at Mitsue, looked at the card again, and looked at Mitsue again. Finally he grunted and nodded towards the door.

The wedding was a nice affair, given the circumstances. The

children from Mitsue's Sunday school sang. Their voices were like a spring rain, and Mitsue let it wash over her.

After the ceremony, everyone went to a Chinese restaurant. They had to eat in a hurry as they had to be home by the eight o'clock curfew. The two RCMP officers followed along to the restaurant too. At seven-thirty they said, "Time's up." Everyone got their jackets and went home. What else could they do?

There was no honeymoon. The next day, Mitsue moved into the rooming house with Hideo's family. She hated living there. There were five bedrooms in the house on Jackson Street, just a few blocks off Powell Street. Hideo's parents slept on the main floor beside the kitchen. On the second floor there were two bedrooms and a large bathroom. Hideo and Mitsue had one room and Hideo's sister June had the other. The third floor had three more rooms, which were rented out. When Mitsue moved in, there was one man in each room. They were all labourers who worked at the mills and stayed in the house when they had days off. The house was constantly dirty. She would spend all day cleaning the men's clothes, their sheets, and their rooms.

Mitsue washed the men's clothes with a scrubbing brush. It would take hours to get the grime out of their work shirts and pants and underwear. She'd scrub them with powdered detergent, hang-dry them, press them with a stove iron, fold them, and leave them on each man's bed. She never did get a thank you, at least not from the men. Hideo's mother, Wari, was grateful for the help. She had been doing all the work by herself for so long. Hideo's father, Hanpei, was hardly ever around. He worked at the lumber camp, half a day's drive away, and would come back to Vancouver on the weekends. He was gruff and liked to gamble, so most weekends he wasn't around either. Hanpei hardly knew his son. They never really talked.

Mitsue toiled away at the rooming house. Breakfast, clean, lunch, clean, dinner, clean. Hideo went back to work at the paper mill, so she was often alone with Wari. Wari was a sharp woman. She had spent her life running a boarding house after working on the farm back in Japan. She had never gone to school. She worked every day. And she was often alone with boarders, so she had to be tough. She was very different than Mitsue's mother. It took Mitsue a while to get accustomed to living with Wari, who only spoke when she had to give orders.

Mitsue was able to stay on at Mrs. Yamamoto's dress shop. She went in every other weekday. White customers were not coming around as much, and Mrs. Yamamoto was becoming worried about her business. She was widowed and had no family in Canada aside from a cousin who worked at a mine up north. She was always looking for information about what was happening to the people who had already been sent away from Vancouver. Where were they going? What was it like? Nobody really knew. It was all just speculation in those early days. Only a few people had actually been evacuated. They had been sent to ghost towns in B.C.'s interior. The thought of living in a ghost town terrified Mrs. Yamamoto. Night and day, she thought about this.

Notices of evacuation were everywhere. Everyone feared opening their mailbox. A clearing was underway. It was systematic and ruthless. It was coming for everyone.

Some received as little as two hours' notice to leave their home. When her time came a few months later, Mrs. Yamamoto was one of the lucky ones. She was given one week. Mitsue helped her pack. She gave most of her fabric to a *hakujin* family, good customers who lived just down the street.

When Mitsue was packing clothes she noticed several canning jars in the bedroom. There was cash on the bed. Mitsue never asked but she guessed Mrs. Yamamoto was planning to bury money in her backyard. Mrs. Yamamoto didn't know who to turn to, didn't know who to trust.

The day came for Mrs. Yamamoto to report to Hastings Park. She walked through the gates, feeling like a prisoner. Everyone was quiet and hung their heads. Cots were assigned in the livestock building. The cattle stalls were still up. Cows had just been in them. The troughs were still there. Hay lay on the ground, smelling of manure and urine and blood.

Some people had put up sheets in the stalls for a little privacy. But mostly they were just sitting on their cots with nothing to do. There was a big mess hall in one of the other buildings. Gruel was being served, but no one ate. More than two thousand people were confined in that park. Armed guards patrolled the premises. People arrived completely unprepared for the brutality of the situation. It was worse than any rumour that had been conjured up. Not in their wildest dreams had Japanese Canadians thought they'd be locked up in cattle stalls among lice and manure. These were honest people: mothers and fathers and children and grandparents. Their lives had been stolen. Their sole crime: being Japanese.

Mitsue thought: *this can't get any worse*. She was wrong.

On February 26, 1942, Justice Minister Louis St.-Laurent gave the B.C. Security Commission absolute power to implement the evacuation. The commission moved with ruthless efficiency. By March 4, a committee of three men was empowered to remove all individuals of Japanese origin, Canadian or not, from the hundred-mile coastal region. They were efficient and brutal. Within twenty days of the first committee meeting, more than fifteen hundred Japanese Canadians had been shipped to Hastings Park. Many more were in a queue. In all, over twenty-one thousand would be taken away.

There had not been a single reported incident of conspiracy or treason among the Japanese in Canada. No judicial proceedings took place. There were no Blue Ribbon Committees. There was very little public debate at all. Not a single institution came to the defence of the Japanese.

With radios confiscated, it was difficult to know what was happening. Mitsue's stomach was in knots throughout the early spring of 1942. Folks were moving out all the time, making their way to Hastings Park. Some went to ghost towns in the interior, some to road camps in Ontario. Some families were going to the prairies. Everyone knew it was just a matter of time before they were removed.

As May turned to June, Mitsue's spirits began to lift. The Americans had won the Battle of Midway. If the Japanese military was not a threat, certainly she would not be sent away. If there was no national security issue, then they could just go on with their lives. Her father would get his boats back and she would not have to leave Vancouver with her new husband. If a Japanese invasion was now impossible, surely there would be no more internment. She allowed herself to think that she could just carry on, forget that this whole ugly episode had ever happened.

But the resettlements continued. Her dad was right. Canada just wanted them out. It was as simple as that. And then Mitsue's time came. Just like everyone else, she got a letter by registered mail. That is how she learned she was being uprooted. She didn't feel shock. She had seen it happen to so many friends. It was happening everywhere. She felt numb as she opened the envelope.

The letter said that her family could stay together if they went to the sugar-beet work camps on the prairies. Mitsue took the letter to her parents' house. They had received a similar letter just the day before. For the final time, they all sat in the living room of the Celtic row house—this time to make the most important decision of their lives. In the end there wasn't much to decide. They had to stay together. It was the only thing that mattered.

Pat was livid. How could this be happening to them? They had done nothing wrong. They were all Canadian. But Yosuke was prepared. He looked each family member in the eye in turn. He looked at these people who were close to his heart and whispered: "*Shikata-ga-nai*." It can't be helped. He whispered it so they would listen closely.

And that was that. They would have to do their best and cling to their dignity. *Shikata-ga-nai*. Mitsue repeated the words in her head over and over. She had heard the phrase before, but on that terrible day it felt like the finest gift she had ever received. If you can't help it, you have to survive it.

That night after dinner, they filled out the request form to stay together as a family. They would try to go to southern Alberta. Hideo took both replies to the post office the very next morning. The forms went to the Security Commission for the government to decide. Their fate was no longer in their own hands.

The fields of Alberta were empty. The men had all gone off to fight. The war had cut off the sugar supply from Southeast Asia and the government had to ration sugar consumption, so Alberta farmers started to grow sugar beets. It was hard work and the province had too few workers to do it. The Japanese were their only option. Alberta begrudgingly accepted them.

While the Sakamotos waited to find out their fate, life went on as usual. Of course, the evacuation was always on everyone's mind like a bad headache, leaving them feeling hollowed out.

Mitsue tried her best to focus on the tasks at hand as she waited to see if her family would be permitted to stay together. The men in the rooming house still needed their three square meals. The bedding still needed to be washed, and the ironing and cleaning had to be done. For the next few weeks Mitsue went back to work. Hideo went back to the lumberyard. He thought he might as well earn some money in B.C. while he was able.

Mitsue didn't like to be left alone. Powell Street didn't feel safe anymore. She half expected a brick to come crashing through the window. But they were going to need the money. She was left with Wari to manage the house. Since Wari was unwell that week, Mitsue ended up working especially hard as she packed up as much as she could in preparation for their evacuation date.

Finally, the wait was over. The Security Commission granted passage to southern Alberta to Yosuke, Tomi, Pat, Mary, and Susanne. They'd be on two farms in Coaldale.

Nobody had any idea where Coaldale was. They tried to look it up on various maps of Canada, but it was too small to be included. *Coaldale.* Mitsue said it in her mind a few times. It didn't sound like a very nice place. But at least they would be together. They actually felt lucky. Almost grateful.

The fog of confusion had begun to lift, but the reality was painful. Mitsue went to her parents' house to talk about what they would take to Coaldale. Susanne was in her bedroom crying. She had just started at Point Grey Junior High and had been elected vice-president of her class. Teachers and children alike recognized her keen intellect. When the order came, none of her teachers had asked her about her fate. Susanne wondered what was behind their indifference. Her school friends seemed unaware of what was happening to her. Just before the order came, she was to have gone into the city with her class to see the *Ice Capades.* She was in the schoolyard as everyone boarded the bus.

"Why aren't you coming, Susanne?"

"I can't. I have a curfew."

"Why?"

"Because I'm Japanese."

They couldn't understand. Neither could she.

Susanne had known for some time that her days at school were numbered. She was determined to continue her education in Alberta. A few days after the order came, she went to see the counsellor for a transfer slip. No questions were asked, and the counsellor barely looked at her as she signed the paper. Susanne left, clutching that form like it was gold. It would allow her to continue school wherever she ended up. That done, she went to Miss McKillop, her history teacher, and told her that she had to leave. Miss McKillop just stood up and told the class that Susanne was moving away. That was it. Susanne said goodbye and, as her classmates looked on, she left, feeling like an enemy alien. She walked down the empty hall with tears pooling in her eyes. What were her classmates thinking? Why were they silent?

Why didn't anyone say something? Their silence left her with an uneasy sadness.

Yosuke and Tomi were devastated to see Susanne's studies interrupted. It was, to them, the worst theft possible. Susanne read anything and everything. She loved to learn; she took in new knowledge like Pat took in fish from the sea.

Mitsue was supposed to go home on account of the curfew, but she was trying her best to console Susanne, so she decided to stay the night. It was the first time she had slept in her old house since she got married. After dinner, she helped Mary with the dishes while Yosuke and Tomi spoke with Susanne in the living room. Susanne finally went to bed.

As the dishes dried, Mitsue watched her parents hugging outside Susanne's bedroom. They were both crying. Education was the most important thing they could give their children. It was their only way forward, their only way up. But now their little girl, the most intellectually gifted of their children, was being robbed of her chance. Yosuke believed that the only thing that couldn't be taken away was what you put in your mind.

On her way home the next morning, Mitsue stopped at a store to order the boxes they needed to take their things to the prairies. The boxes were wood, about three feet by two feet, and no more than three feet high. Some stores in Little Tokyo were only selling boxes now—that's all anyone wanted. Boxes and food. Each person was only allowed to bring 150 pounds, which added up fast. The government suggested packing blankets, a sewing machine, and cooking supplies. That was close to 150 pounds right there.

Scarcity leads to tough decisions. Should they take family albums or extra rice? Letters from family in Japan or an extra blanket? They were in survival mode and didn't have the luxury of being sentimental. You couldn't eat pictures, and letters wouldn't keep you warm on a cold winter night unless you burned them. They packed up the belongings they were leaving behind and took them to the Japanese centre. Each family was allowed a small storage area. Every last picture they had was packed into boxes, along with family heirlooms and letters. They put their kimonos into boxes too. Yosuke and Pat packed their fishing nets. What they needed to survive came with them. But their hearts were put away and stacked in the Japanese centre. It was an appropriate place to house their hearts.

Once each family had filled their allotted area with what they were leaving behind, the men of Celtic came to board up the building and lock it up. It wasn't until they put a chain along the front door that the families understood this was a goodbye. Those families on Celtic Lane—the Osekis, the Nakamuras, the Uyedas, the Ishikawas, the Nagatas, the Yamamotos, the Endos, the Omotanis, the Adachis, the Kadonagas, the Yoshiharas, the Shintanis, the Mikis, the Minamimayes, the Yasudas, the Charas, the Kanos, the Marumotos, the Yamashitas, the Shintanis—were one extended family. They gathered for a final photo before leaving.

Yosuke locked up the family house. Mitsue went back to the boarding house to help Wari pack up. Hideo and Hanpei were boarding up the windows. So many buildings in Little Tokyo were like that by then, boarded up and empty. They packed what was

needed into the boxes that Mitsue had ordered. Hideo carefully nailed each one closed. Mitsue had made sure to get at least one that had a tin lining so they could take rice, since they were not sure if they'd be able to get rice once they reached the prairies. Hideo had to help Mitsue pour bag after bag of rice into that box. He wrote *Sakamoto* in Japanese kanji characters on each box.

Mitsue did take one thing for herself, though. She just couldn't leave her wedding pictures behind. After Wari and Hanpei went to bed, she hid the photos, folded up in blankets to keep them safe and sound. Mitsue told Hideo what she had done and he didn't say a word. He just walked over to the box, put the lid on, and nailed it shut. Then he smiled and went back to his own packing.

CHAPTER 6

Ralph's War

Ralph clung to the side of the hill. He took one last look back at his rifle and dropped his knife.

Scanning the trees, he peeked over the cliff and saw five men standing up. One man's shirt was completely blood soaked and he held his right shoulder with his bloodied left hand.

They were out of options. A megaphone from across the valley made that clear. "The war is over. I give you safe passage to surrender. Do not die."

Ralph and the rest of the Canadians emerged with their hands in the air and followed the sound of the megaphone down the hill. As the enemy came into view, the Canadians were astonished. The Japanese had moved in under cover of darkness. The fight had been thirteen against three hundred.

Two very young-looking Japanese soldiers ordered Ralph and six other men to line up against a rock wall and to stand in place with bayonets pointed at their faces. Both soldiers had fresh blood on them. Japanese soldiers were everywhere. Many stopped and gave the Canadians a hard look.

The commander stood atop a small mound. He still had the megaphone in his left hand. He stared at the men for some time, then drew his katana sword. He took slow, short steps towards the prisoners, never once breaking eye contact with them.

Three Japanese soldiers all had their guns drawn. Their backs to the wet rock wall, each Canadian watched the bayonets closely, knowing the Japanese would save their bullets. The commander stood three feet in front of them, gripping his sword. He went down the line, asking each for his name and rank. Ralph was the last in line.

"Ralph Augustus MacLean, Lance Corporal, E30382."

"Where are you men coming from?"

Nobody responded, prompting the commander to raise his sword to his waist. The curved blade caught the light through the trees.

"Palm Villa," someone down the line said. "We were based out of Palm Villa."

This brought a smile to the commander's face, which in turn left a knot in the stomach of each of the seven men. They knew very well what his smile meant.

The commander looked over his shoulder and gave an order in Japanese. He was through with these men. He sheathed his blade, turned, and made his way into his tent. The three guards and their bayonets stayed put.

With nothing more for the Canadians to do or say, exhaustion took over. Too weary to care, Ralph leaned against the rock wall and promptly fell asleep. He had barely closed his eyes in three whole days.

He awoke to a guard tying his wrists with barbed wire. He was ordered to his feet and told to move. The other men, tied to one another, were moving now too.

And so began the march. They made their way down a long and winding trail that cut through the heavy brush overgrowth. The men walked in single file with their hands out in front of them. They were careful to stay as even as possible; any jerking action caused the barbed wire to cut deep and elicited groans down the whole line.

The situation was difficult for the soldier who had taken shrapnel across his right shoulder. The others tried to keep him alert and on his feet. The guards would yell bloody murder if the men slowed down, stumbled, or spoke. They let their bayonets do most of the talking—raising them to face level whenever there was a missed step or when a groan slipped out.

Three miles down the trail, the front guard belted out "Halt!" as he turned and raised his right hand. All the men stopped. He lowered his hand and ordered the men to sit down on the side of the trail. They tried their best to do so, but the wounded man's legs buckled, sending him sprawling while the other six grimaced in pain. Ralph felt delirious. He had not had any food since the two bites of corned beef days earlier. He had not had any water since then either. The men looked at each other. They were all thinking about water. The white spit at the corners of their mouths betrayed their desperate thirst.

As they looked around, one of them gestured with his chin across the trail. Five men, hands tied together with barbed wire exactly as they were, lay slumped over. Each had a bayonet gash to the stomach. Their deaths must have been slow and horrific. Even in death, their faces could not hide their torment. It was as if they were still screaming. Some eyes were open, some were shut. Ralph scanned them, looking for a familiar face, dreading that he'd see one. His companions all thought the same thing at the same time. Were they about to be stabbed to death?

In Ralph's mouth was the metallic taste of fear. It was as if he had eaten nails. Three guards emerged from the bush. One was doing up his zipper. The fourth was walking past the dead Canadians, inspecting them with disconcerting familiarity.

"Fuck," one of the captives whispered. Another was breathing heavily. Panic was setting in. Ralph flashed a cold stare down the line. He said nothing but the look meant, *Easy, boys. Let's not lose our heads here.*

"Up!" the guard yelled once he'd closed his zipper. The fourth guard sauntered over, his eyes as dead as the fallen Canadians. The seven men all watched his bayonet. It was clean as a whistle. His pant leg, however, was caked in blood. He slowly walked over to the man at the end of the line. No one looked at his face. He moved on to the second, the third, and the fourth. The fifth man was the wounded one. The guard stood beside him for an eternity. The man kept his head down and his hand shook as he gripped his wounded arm. Ralph—who was standing next to him—closed his eyes and offered a prayer. The Japanese soldier spit and moved on—past Ralph and the seventh Canadian.

"Move!" he yelled. The march continued. A minor miracle.

By nightfall, they reached their destination. As they crested a large hill, they saw a mass of men making their way into a large structure like a coliseum. It was too dark to know for sure, but Ralph thought he had seen it before. As they made their way down towards it, the structure came into focus.

They entered, the bright yellow and red lights still shining brightly announcing the Happy Valley Race Track. The irony was painful.

A stench hit the seven men as they reached the bleachers and the track revealed itself. Men were laid out everywhere. Some were dead, some still alive. Ralph's eyes searched in vain for a medical station, a water line, or a mess hall. The lead guard just motioned with his rifle butt for them to move down the stairs onto the track. They made their way onto the field, stepping gingerly around the bodies, living and dead. Still bound, they had to be careful not to trip and send their whole line sprawling.

Each face they saw offered a dreadful story of defeat, terror, or death. Mostly the men were numb. Sheer exhaustion had dampened their ability to feel, to think, or to act. Without saying a word, the seven men found a clearing large enough for all of them. They lay down in unison. Ralph stared at the sky. It was a cloudy humid night. He offered a Merry Christmas to no one in particular.

As night fell in the Happy Valley Race Track, the war seemed to be over. But the men's battle was just beginning.

Boxing Day brought little reprieve. Ralph awoke to a shot of pain up his left side. One of the men in the middle of the sleeping pack rolled over in his sleep and the three men to his left paid the price. They writhed in pain as the barbed wire dug deeper into their wrists.

Some of the prisoners were marched to the streets surrounding Happy Valley Race Track and ordered to clean up the bodies. They were given matches and told to build a fire. The bodies betrayed their brutal demise, wrists tied, eyes gouged, ears sliced off. These men had died in the worst of ways. As the fire grew around them, the scarred bodies returned to the fetal position. They hissed, blackened, and burned.

Amid death, there were unexpected tales of survival. One man came in on a stretcher with maggots falling out of a gaping hole in his face. He had been captured, tied up, shot several times, and left for dead in a ditch. Another poor soul was carried in by a fellow Canadian soldier. He was unable to walk because his private parts had been mutilated by Japanese bayonets. That these men had survived without medical attention for days on end was simply miraculous. The search parties that found them spread the stories; they were rays of hope. If those guys could survive, anyone could.

Then came the news: the Canadians were to be at the western exit at eight o'clock that night, ready to ship out to North Point Camp. All hope ended there.

The men were loaded onto cargo trucks. Canvas enclosed the entire cabin, leaving them in pitch black. Ralph closed his eyes and let his utter exhaustion sweep him away. He awoke to a sudden stop that slammed him into the fellow sleeping beside him. Moments later, the back door dropped open.

"Out!" was the order.

Ralph got to his feet, back hunched. He was not sure if he'd slept for twenty minutes or twenty hours. The sunlight burned his eyes as he jumped off the truck. He put his hand up, blocking his face. He took five steps past a barbed wire fence.

"Ralphie!"

The voice was unmistakable. Ralph opened his eyes, glad he could blame the tears on the hot sun.

"Ralphie, jeez, I thought you were a goner. A goner for sure!" Deighton said as he hugged his friend.

The sight of transport trucks rolling into North Point's main entrance was the only thing that could put a smile on the POWs' faces. As Ralph looked around, his stomach sank. He saw garbage strewn everywhere in the parade square. Body parts, just limbs and torsos, were piled up at the other end of the camp. As the smell of rotting flesh hit him, he doubled over and threw up.

"I know. The smell is terrible. They hope to have it dealt with this week." Deighton was apologizing as if it were a messy living room. "Come on. I've been saving you a spot to sleep."

They made their way through the camp. Deighton explained the layout as they walked.

"We don't have any toilets, so see there where that man is climbing up on that wall?" Deighton pointed to a stone wall to the far south end. "That's our toilet. You just do your business right over the wall into the water. That's where the smell is coming from. There must be a hundred dead Chinese just floating in that water. It's terrible, Ralphie, they are all bloated and shot up. Lots of cattle in there too. The wounded guys tie themselves to that wall before they go so they don't fall. If you fall in, there is no coming back."

The two of them made their way past a long building made of cinderblock.

"That's the mess hall. But it is shit," he said in a hushed tone. "They are feeding us just mouldy rice. More maggots than rice, really. The only meat I have seen since I got here is half a fucking fish head. A *fish head*. I got one cheek and one eyeball—the rest just bone and skin. Eat what you can, Ralphie. It's bad here. Real bad." The end of the mess hall opened to a dirt square with a series of huts along the north perimeter. Ralph followed Deighton into one of the huts.

"There are no beds. My spot is over there." Deighton pointed.

Ralph took three steps into the hut and felt two drops: one on his shoulder, one on his head. He thought it odd that there was a leak in the roof; it had not rained in the past few days. The raindrop on his shirt moved. He wiped his shoulder and his head. A few men down the way chuckled.

Ralph looked up. The ceiling was alive.

"Bedbugs. They are the scourge of North Point," Deighton said. "Well, them and the lice."

Deighton took off his shirt. Red spots covered his torso. "Look at the seams of my shirt."

Ralph focused in the hazy light of the hut. He took a closer look and then snapped his head back when he saw a dozen bugs scatter on his friend's shirt as they were exposed. At this, even Deighton laughed.

"Can't do a damn thing about 'em, Ralph. They are even rewarding us with smokes if we catch these bloody things. It's no use. We just can't beat these little buggers."

Ralph didn't have a pack to throw down, so he sat down on the makeshift bedding to inspect it. It was held together by a thick canvas, but large holes exposed coconut shells, the hair sticking out like a ragged scalp.

He and Deighton went out for a walk around the parade square in the middle of the camp. It was the only thing they could do, though they had to be careful to conserve energy. Deighton had been in the camp for three days and had lost a pound a day.

The officers fared far better. They had their own cabin and were offered real food and American cigarettes. Coffee, even. As the officers finished their smokes, they'd casually flick the butts to the ground, just as they would have done before the war. But their men would scramble on the ground for them. Ralph wondered, if it was this bad on day three, where would they be in a month?

As dinner time rolled around there were rumours of meat. The men made their way into the mess hall, just an open room with a few tables. The kitchen consisted of three kettles and a transport truck hubcap that had been scavenged off the adjacent road. There was one large rice pot and no plates. The men lined up for one scoop of mouldy rice custard and a slice of rancid whale meat. No one knew if they were better off eating it or leaving it.

There were no seats. Ralph and Deighton found an empty corner against the wall and slid down onto their backsides, careful not to drop any food.

"Bon appétit, Garbage Can," Deighton said, shooting Ralph a sly smile. The familiarity almost brought Ralph to tears for the second time that day.

They ate in silence. The food tasted terrible. When they were done, they made their way back to their hut. The Japanese guards counted them off to make sure nobody had escaped, and then it was lights-out. Ralph dropped onto his bedding. He could feel it crawling. His stomach was in one big empty knot. He felt demonstrably weaker and he had only been on the grounds of North Point for fifteen hours.

Ralph woke up the next day covered in bites from head to toe. He opened his shirt and peeled the seams back—there were the lice, nestled in.

The men gathered in the parade square to be counted off and get some physical activity. The mess hall was serving more slop: mouldy rice and a three-inch square of bread.

But at least the routine of Ralph's new life had begun. In a strange way, he felt comforted by it. His clock was reset to army time. It beat the chaos of battle. Lice beat bullets. Sleep beat marching.

The second week that Ralph was at North Point, the men were awoken in the middle of the night by an alarm over the camp's speaker. Everyone thought at first it was an air raid alarm. A Japanese guard kicked their door in. He slowly walked the hall. He was counting.

"Out!" he ordered.

The men lined up in the parade square as they did every morning and evening. They were counted. They were counted again.

And again. And again. Whispers down the line made it clear Sergeant Payne and a few others were missing. They had hopped the fence and disappeared into the water basin. The men they'd left behind spent all night in the pouring rain being counted.

Those who had tried to escape didn't make it far. After six hours, as dawn was breaking, five gunshots rang out from behind the mess hall.

As the remaining men made their way through the line for their morning serving of rice stew, the cooks noticed there were five fewer men from the Winnipeg Grenadiers.

A commanding officer approached Ralph's table. He spoke to the men, passing word down that the Japanese had instituted a new plan. Each man would be assigned to a group of ten. Should any man within the ten attempt to escape, the nine others would be summarily executed.

This rule, and the fact that there really was nowhere for a tall white soldier to hide on the island of Hong Kong, largely put an end to any further escape attempts. The men had seen too many pointless deaths. Nobody wanted nine more on their conscience.

Everyone at North Point was dying. The Japanese authorities were withholding adequate food and necessary medicine. They forced the men to grovel in filth, to wade in bare feet into human excrement to relieve themselves. Men were aging days by the minute, weeks by the hour. The days dragged on. The only thing that happened quickly was weight loss.

Daily scenes of violence ate away at their souls. Starving Chinese beggars would risk death to approach the fence line in hopes of selling an orange or a pair of sandals. Ralph saw one boy, maybe eight or nine, approach the fence with what looked like a dirty blanket. He held it out to two prisoners as they walked along the well-worn path around the parade square. The soldiers tried to shoo him away before the tower guard saw him. He raised the blanket as they passed him, trying to speak. His tiny voice was drowned out by gunfire. Ralph ducked. When he looked up again, the boy was slumped on top of his blanket. A few minutes later, an elderly Chinese lady came running towards him, howling. She pulled the dead boy away on the bloodied blanket.

Some men could not accept the new reality. Ralph feared that his buddy Deighton was one of them. Bedbugs were *not* falling onto their heads from the ceiling, they were *not* eating maggots and rice, they had *not* lost twenty pounds in a few short weeks. They were *not* POWs. They were *not* dying. They could not transition into survival mode.

Ralph knew self-preservation cold. It was the only gift his father had ever given him. From the moment he was captured, survival was the only thing on his mind. He took no unnecessary risks. He kept his head down and ate everything and anything that was put in front of him.

No one was spared. By the summer of 1942, Ralph, like the rest of the men, was wasting away. Their skin stuck to their bones; their faces were drawn and gaunt. The weakened men could not ward off the terrible diseases that lurked in the filth and grime around them. By summer, the worst enemy was not hunger or their Japanese captors—it was dysentery and diphtheria.

Sleep was impossible. Most of the men had long since stopped sleeping in their infested beds, opting to huddle together in groups of six or seven on the cold concrete floor. The bedbugs would still get them, but the lice bit less on the floor. The men's feet radiated pain all night. They called it electric feet. Ralph tried soaking his feet in cold water for some relief but the shooting pain would always be back before he made his way from the front of the hut to his group of companions on the floor. The shooting pain was so bad the men felt like they were being electrocuted from the toes up.

One day Deighton held his spoon to his mouth, stared at the milky white slop, closed his eyes tight, and forced it in. Two slow bites was all he could handle. His gag reflex kicked in and the rice dropped onto his lap. It was his fourth try. He choked and dry-heaved. He would have vomited, but there was nothing in his stomach to throw up.

He sat at the table and wept. He knew if he didn't eat he would perish. Diphtheria had taken hold of him. His throat was so inflamed it was almost completely shut. Some men choked to death in their sleep. The infections had run rampant through Deighton's body: his nose, cheeks, neck, and scrotum were covered in gaping ulcers. Ralph had fallen asleep every night for the past week to the wheezing gasps of his buddy as he tried his best to keep him warm on the miserable concrete floor.

Each morning, Deighton's eyes had become more distant. The faraway look was the beginning of the end. It was the look of the living staring into the realm of the dead. The eyes always went first. The body quickly followed.

Deighton dropped his spoon. He kept his head slouched over his clay bowl.

"I'm gone, Ralph. I'm gone," he whispered.

Ralph knew his buddy needed out. He would not last another night. Straight away, he went to the infirmary to plead with the doctor.

"There is a truck taking some of the worst out tomorrow. Let me take a look at you too, Rifleman," the doctor said.

"I'm fine," Ralph lied as he opened his mouth. He was not there for himself. The orderly took one look and rushed out of the room. He came back out of breath, holding a bottle full of white powder.

"Take this now."

"I'm fine," Ralph repeated, but he did as he was told.

"You are *both* going. Be at the front gate at oh-eight-hundred hours with Deighton."

Ralph hoped Deighton would still be alive in nineteen hours.

Electric feet kept Ralph awake that whole night. It felt as though his nerves were hooked up to a car battery. He was huddled right beside Deighton, who didn't move at all. Ralph looked hard

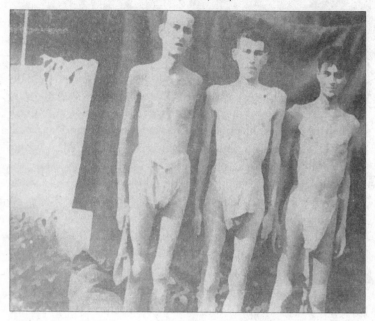

in the dark to see if his friend's chest was moving up and down. He couldn't tell. He could hear a man choking at the other end of the hut. The man wheezed loudly and struggled, and Ralph heard him take his last gasp. He was one of eight men to die that night alone.

Ralph and Deighton lined up at the front gate right after breakfast. Deighton had gone another meal without eating. Five men in stretchers had already been placed there. One had not survived the fifty-yard journey from the infirmary to the front gate. Six other men strong enough to stand were behind them, all waiting for the transport truck. Ralph and Deighton stood side by side at the rear. A few men fell into line behind them.

Ralph heard the truck roar up to the front gate but had to turn to his left to see it. It was then he noticed he could no longer see out of his right eye.

The truck was a military transport. The cab was covered with canvas. One Japanese soldier opened the tailgate and jumped out of the back, followed by another. They loaded the four stretchers, dumping the dead man's body onto the ground and loading that empty stretcher.

"In!" the Japanese soldier ordered the first man as he held onto the ladder and tried to drag his weak body up the required four feet.

Ralph did a quick calculation. With the men in stretchers taking up space, it was going to be a tight fit.

"Next!"

A second soldier tried to board, but he slipped and cracked his jaw on the open tailgate. He was out cold. Ralph and two others lifted him in. They were the only men strong enough to hike themselves into the cab unassisted.

Deighton and Ralph slowly made their way to the front of the line. The guard pointed at Ralph. "You next!" he said, giving Ralph a hard shove as he climbed in.

Ralph scrambled into the truck and turned with his hand outstretched for his friend. "That's it!" the guard yelled as he closed the tailgate.

Ralph's left eye locked onto Deighton's. "Grab my hand!"

Deighton raised his hand and took a step forward. The guard cross-checked him with his rifle, sending him sprawling into the men in line behind him. They all fell. Ralph's hand was still out when the back door slammed shut.

"There's room! There's room in here!" Ralph pleaded. His one good eye was trained on Deighton. The truck's motor revved to life. Both guards were now in the front cabin. The truck started to pull away.

"Hurry!" Ralph's body was half out the back as he screamed at Deighton. With a gasp, Deighton got up and made a lunge for Ralph's hand. Their hands met and he got one foot on the truck's back ladder.

"C'mon, Deighton!" Ralph cried.

Their faces were now inches apart. He could hear Deighton wheeze as he struggled to get his second foot off the ground. Their hands clutched each other. Then the truck hit a bump and Deighton slipped away. Ralph watched his friend hit the ground and roll to a stop. His face was buried in the dirt. He didn't move.

"Deighton!" Ralph cried, as two of the men in the truck pulled him back into the safety of his seat.

"There was room. You bastards. There was room!" Tears of rage burned Ralph's eyes.

When he came to, Ralph didn't know if he was alive or dead, awake or dreaming. He could hear what sounded like nurses tending to wounded men. But he could neither move nor see anything. His world was completely black. He was unsure of where he was. He lay there like that for some time, listening, then lost consciousness again.

He woke again to someone bandaging his feet. A nurse? The pain seared up his legs. But he was relieved—at least the pain confirmed he was alive. His mind immediately went to Deighton. He could feel tears roll down his cheeks.

"Doctor, this one is conscious, I think," he heard a nurse say.

Ralph waited in anticipation, unable to respond or ask what had happened to him, unable to ask if they knew anything about Deighton—though he didn't want to know the answer.

A doctor was by his side. "Son, diphtheria has blinded you. Can you move your right toe for me?"

Ralph tried with all his might, to no avail.

"We are going to give you some medicine," the doctor informed him. A needle was plunged into his thigh. He didn't feel a thing.

"We've giving you a shot. You should know we're only giving it to the ones that have a fighting chance. You do, son. So fight, boy. Fight with all your might."

Ralph did just that.

After three weeks of darkness, Ralph awoke and could make out the number "3" on the foot of his bed. It was—and continued to be—the most beautiful thing he had ever seen. Letting out a moan was his way of saying: *I'm alive*. A tiny circle of light slowly became blurred beds and a window, which eventually became the ward he was in. It consisted of fourteen beds, seven to each side, with one window between the third and fourth beds. Each bed had a skeleton of a man in it.

Two nurses approached. Ralph could only make out their white blouses and long hair. An angelic voice informed him he was in the Bowen Road Military Hospital on Hong Kong Island. Ralph thought the next time he'd hear such a beautiful voice would be when he reached the pearly gates.

But Bowen Hospital was no heavenly palace. It was a series of four five-storey buildings that had been heavily shelled during the battle. The building had withstood the bombardment, but when it was overrun, most of the patients were bayonetted in their beds. The two nurses who stood in front of Ralph had been brutally raped and beaten. Some nurses had died. Those who lived continued to assist the wounded soldiers.

Ralph was in and out of consciousness for some time. His memory later was of a series of fleeting objects and sounds. A bedpan. A needle. A cry. Over time, the daily injections brought life back to his limbs. The dishes of mutton, oranges, peach jam on bread, and hard-boiled duck eggs dimmed the bolts of pain that spiralled through his feet and legs. He would learn to walk all over again, one step at a time.

Ralph was back from the dead.

After eight weeks in Bowen, Ralph was told that he was going to be sent back. He would be receiving his last injection. The doctor was apologetic. He knew what he was sending his patient back to, but Ralph was at a distance from death now. Many others were not. They needed the beds.

The doctor wished desperately that he could do more. Ralph could see that much in his eyes. He'd been playing God since the outbreak of the war, deciding which man got the medicine and which man was too far gone. His decisions saved some men and condemned others. Ralph could see the weight of this on his slouching shoulders.

"This should hold you over. The Japs won't let us send the meds into the camps. I hope I don't see you again, Ralph," the doctor said in a thick Scottish accent that reminded Ralph of the folks back home.

Ralph left Bowen Hospital with a heavy heart. He felt like he was set to face the cold, bitter North Atlantic wind after a brief reprieve by a warm fire. He knew the rest of his journey was going to be nasty and brutish. His only salvation was that it might be short.

He was sent back to Shamshuipo.

Ralph got off the truck. He knew everything that was about to hit him. He walked through the front gate with eyes wide open. He knew the lice would be back. He knew the pangs of hunger were a few days away. He knew he'd likely contract another deficiency-related disease: beriberi, dysentery, or ulcers. He knew he'd see more brutality. He knew each step he took brought him closer to that very real hell. What he didn't know was just how devastatingly lonely life would be without Deighton.

He had come full circle, but the camp was a rundown shell of its former self, as were the men who inhabited it. It had been looted after the Japanese took it. Barbed wire had been strung all around the huts, and machine guns were set up on all four corners. The only familiar sights at the camp were the Chinese barbers and shoe shiners. Most now wore Japanese military uniforms.

Ralph approached the first group of men he saw. "Did you hear anything about Deighton?" he asked no one in particular. The men were glad to see Ralph alive. Everyone knew how he and Deighton had been separated. The other men in line that day had seen Ralph reach out to save his buddy. Nobody wanted to be the one to let him know.

There was a long silence. "He died the night you left. His body just gave out," said a voice from the back of the group.

Ralph closed his eyes and nodded. He remembered the promise they had made to each other after enlisting. Deighton had made good on it. Even in death, he'd had his buddy's back. Without his tears for Deighton, Ralph would have been carried out of Bowen Hospital in a bodybag.

That night he huddled on the cement floor of his hut with five other guys. He hoped they thought his shivers were from the cold. He didn't fool anyone. He'd been a prisoner for almost a year. In that time, he had lost half his weight, his sight, the ability to move, and now, his very best friend. And yet, he knew there was more to lose.

Almost immediately, the pangs of hunger revisited him, though he was in much better shape than most. During three of the eight weeks at Bowen he had had at least two square meals a day.

Combining North Point and Shamshuipo into one camp had created a desperate situation. While the dysentery had abated, all the men were in the throes of starvation. They scavenged for anything they could find. If a man could get his hands on a rat, he was lucky. To make matters worse, the men's minds dwelled on home cooking. It was the worst form of self-torture. They'd relive memories of meals, review recipes, and rebuke others' pronouncements that their momma made the best Shepherd's pie. They'd choke back tears recounting the smells and tastes of home. Ralph stubbornly refused to partake in this. There was nothing to be gained by it.

When survival is at stake, non-essentials are callously jettisoned. You just keep your heart beating, keep air flowing in and out of your lungs. Put something—anything—into your belly. You can do a lot of things when dignity is set aside. You wrap your dignity up and gently place it in the back of your mind, like a cherished heirloom. It may not see the light of day for months, but the knowledge that it is there is the most important thing you have.

That, and cigarettes.

For Ralph, the need for dignity and the desire for cigarettes collided. Well past the point of having any cigarettes of his own, he would sit day after day watching the Japanese guards and Canadian officers walk the parade grounds pulling on their cigarettes and dropping their butts. *To hell with it*, he thought, and made his way over to a tossed butt. He got halfway across the field. He could see the tobacco burning itself out in the grass. It was still good for at least two or three pulls. Five paces away, he stopped dead in his tracks. *To hell with it*, he thought again, and sat down. He watched the cigarette burn down and out.

It was one of the most important decisions he made during the war.

The next morning, Ralph and the others were visited by angels. He would later swear on a stack of bibles that he knew exactly what angels looked like. They came wrapped with a red cross. At perhaps the lowest point in camp morale, when a dozen men were dying every day, angels arrived from the Red Cross. The Japanese kept most of the packages, but each man received one.

Ralph knew that the parcels were from England—the Treacle syrup gave that away. Each parcel weighed fifteen pounds. His was packed with canned meat, dried fruit, condensed milk, and chocolate.

The milk reminded Ralph of the old jersey cow he had back home. He could see her chewing away with her head down, the ocean as a backdrop. The bacon—even dried—reminded him of his mother, standing erect above the old skillet early in the morning, coffee brewing on the stove, quiet so as to not wake the others. A dutiful kiss on the cheek.

The chocolate he saved. He allowed himself one half-inch piece a day. Not for the taste, but for the memories. One bite transported him to the front of the Sumarah General Store with the Uproaders and the Downroaders. Another put him at his aunt's Christmas table, wiping his hands naughtily on her white hand-sewn doily. He saved the last piece for his first memory: skipping rocks and eating chocolate in Charlottetown, just before he and his brother crossed paths with the Chinese launderer. He relished each memory, licking his fingers clean.

Two weeks later, a paper angel came via Switzerland. He could not believe what he held: a letter from his mother. She had put her tender hands on that very paper. He could see a few dents in the strokes on the paper, the pen almost making its way through the page. He knew she had written the letter at the kitchen table without putting a book under the paper. The letter was short and to the point:

You are desperately missed. You are loved.

He smelled the paper, held it close to his face.

He was permitted to write a response. He told his mother he was fine, but his handwriting gave him away. He told her he loved her, and not to worry because he was swell, and to keep the old chin up until they met again.

It was the finest letter he ever penned.

By the summer of 1943, the war had begun to go badly for the Japanese Imperial Army. The death toll was staggering. The Japanese military machine required more able bodies to work in their nation's foundries, shipyards, and mines. They needed steel and coal, bullets and fuel. They needed to arm their soldiers with something—anything—as the Americans inched closer to the island.

And so began the Japanese "draft." The men who were able to walk from one side of a two-lane road to the other won the draft. From one red chalk line to another was about twenty-three steps. The prize was a one-way ticket to Japan.

> Nov. 29/41
> Hongkong,
>
> Dearest Mother
>
> This is Saturday A.M. and I'm not doing anything, this afternoon we have free so I guess Allen Welch and myself will be taking a walk down town!
>
> I'm beginning to see a little more of the town and I guess I might like it after a while. Allen and I usually go to town together and we've been having a fair time considering everything.
>
> We certainly have to watch these Chinese when we buy anything because they'll charge you just about four times the actual value of the article, but we're getting to know them. The poverty in this part of the country (at least) is more than anyone could imagine unless you actually saw it for yourself, people sleeping in the streets and the dirt, but it's not all like that, there is the decent part of the city is pretty nice, and we are treated quite well by most of them. There are Europeans here too, they don't make friends very easily.
>
> Have you heard from Art or Ford lately, send them my address and tell them to write and I'll do my best to answer, it only costs them three cents where it costs me twenty cents, I hope we get free postage soon

Ralph was a winner. He felt a certain relief. He imagined it would be a welcome change. It was their homeland; surely there'd be more food, more provisions, cleaner conditions. How could it get any worse?

At dawn on August 15, 1943, the 276 men who had been able to walk the twenty-three steps the previous evening were marched to the dock beyond the south gate of Shamshuipo. As the gate opened, Ralph made out the ship's name: The SS *Morningstar*. It was an ocean liner. His heart jumped. Maybe, just maybe, things were looking up.

He had never been more wrong in his life.

Even the past two years could not have prepared Ralph for the test he was about to face. He was stepping onto a hell ship, aptly named by the men who would survive the journey.

Ralph was in the middle of the parade march along the dock and up the ship's ramp, so he could see the men in front of him. He knew his way around a ship. As soon as he set foot on the deck, he knew exactly where the line was heading. He braced himself the only way he knew how. He took a deep breath and kept putting one foot in front of the other. Down the stairs the line went, into the guts of the ship. The man in front of him whispered something about beds in the interior cabins. Nope, Ralph thought. They made their way past the mess hall, past the engine room, down another flight of metal steps. The tall men ducked and held the rail. Several slipped on the polished metal track, their bare feet no longer accustomed to walking on metal. Ralph could hear the shouts of a Japanese guard.

"In!" A guttural growl.

He saw the barrel of a mounted machine gun well before he saw the doorway. He knew why it was needed. As it became clear to the man in front of him what was happening, his shoulders slumped and he began to convulse. Ralph realized he must be claustrophobic, and he knew that the man was hyperventilating and about to go into shock. He put a hand on his shoulder.

"Stay steady."

They were only fifteen paces away from the machine gun. As soon as each man stepped through the doorway, he disappeared. They were walking into the void. The ship's cargo hull. Hell.

Ralph's eyes were on the Japanese soldier manning the machine gun. The soldier was perched on a chair, his finger on the trigger. He was in firing position. Ralph was careful not to make eye contact. He knew the man wanted to pull the trigger. The soldier stared at each of them as they passed, daring them, begging them to give him a reason to shoot.

Ralph feared that the man in front of him would provide just that reason. He knew how bullets would spray out of the barrel now a mere ten paces away. They would kill half a dozen men on either side of the target, himself included.

He squeezed the man's shoulder. "Steady. You're going to be okay. Don't panic," he reassured him. "Stay with me."

The man was sobbing silently as they passed the soldier with the gun. Ralph closed his eyes, unsure if he'd ever open them again.

There was no burst from the barrel.

Ralph had no time to feel relief. He opened his eyes to a darkness that went well beyond the absence of light. He could feel the man in front of him move into full hyperventilation, gasping for breath. Ralph lost him in the shuffle as each man searched in vain for a spot to claim. The cargo hull had barely enough room for thirty men to lie down. There were more than one hundred to accommodate.

They were encased in metal. There were no blankets, chairs, or beds. They were cargo. The only concessions they received were a bucket of rice—some cooked, some not—and an empty pail, both lowered down on a rope. With that, the hatch was sealed and the ship's engines roared.

Within hours, the small pail was overflowing with human waste. Ralph's excrement piled up in his pants until they too over-flowed. He moved only when the hatch cracked open and more rice was lowered down. They were worse off than cattle. Worse than rats. Each hour, the air grew thickener with the stink of waste and human decay. Ralph would not see a ray of light for seven days.

The men tried their best to alternate between standing and lying. They tried to ensure that those who became too ill to move were granted space. They tried to allow one another to sleep. They were struggling for their sanity first and their lives second. Bouts of panic would rip through the hull, as contagious as diphtheria. It needed to be quashed or it could overtake them all.

For three days Ralph sat with his head resting on his knees. He went inside himself, as deep as he could go. These were the darkest hours of his life.

The war was not going well for the Japanese, in large part because the Americans owned the sea. The Japanese navy had been sunk months ago during the Battle of Midway. The Japanese Merchant Fleet had also been largely relegated to the bottom of the sea. American submarines prowled the Pacific. They had no way of knowing that the SS Morningstar carried 276 Canadians.

The ship had to dock in Formosa to hide from U.S. subs. The men were permitted to leave the cargo hull for a few hours. While on deck, Ralph spotted a pail of water. He plunged his hands into the pail and splashed his face and drank three gulps from his cupped hands. He could hear boots approaching but he didn't care. He had not had any water in over three days. If he didn't drink, he was going to die. It was worth the beating he knew he was about to take. He felt the soldier pull him up by the back of his baggy shirt, which strained against his neck. The guard spun him around and pushed him against the ship's metal wall. He felt a rail gouge into his lower back. The soldier yelled and hit him twice in the face. Ralph felt the wetness still inside his mouth and tried to hide his smile.

The forced stop rattled many of the men. As they descended back into the cargo hull, they were descending into their own minds. If a submarine torpedo struck, the explosion would rip into the hull. There would be no survivors. By the third day—or at least what seemed to be the third day—Ralph could hear one man praying for just that. "*Send a torpedo. Send a torpedo. Send a torpedo.*" Over and over, for hours on end. Barely audible, but it rang in everyone's ears in the dark of that stifling hull. Finally, mercifully, someone shut the man up.

The second leg of the journey ravaged Ralph's body. For seven days, he sat unable to move, eating only a few handfuls of rice, drinking little more than those three stolen gulps of water. Again he saw no light.

When the shipped docked in Osaka, he was unable to move. His body had withered in the dark and the cold. Feces clung to his back, his buttocks, and his legs. His hair was coarse with salt and urine. Every man was seared by the experience on the hell ship, and Ralph was no exception. Some men were completely broken. Some wept openly as they deboarded.

One thing was for sure: they had left Hong Kong as POWs and arrived in Japan as slave labourers. A contingent of soldiers waited for them at the end of the dock. The first one hundred men were loaded onto cattle cars and immediately shipped to a camp north of Kyoto. The remaining 165 men went by train to Niigata.

The train ride was hours of motion in the dark. The windows were covered with black cloth. One man managed to tear a hole in the cloth and catch a glimpse of the Japanese countryside. He was impressed with what he saw. Ralph didn't see any of it. Too weak to sit up, he lay on the dirty floor for the duration of the trip. When they arrived at the camp, he was put on a stretcher and laid in the courtyard beside several other men.

The camp commandant addressed them, brandishing a Katana sword. The gist of his welcoming remarks was, *You will all live the rest of your days here. You are swine and I'll cut your head off with this sword if you do not obey me or work for me.*

The guards split the men into three groups. The first group went to the foundry. These men would toil next to molten steel and furnaces, spending their days sweating out all the salt they desperately tried to consume while away from the foundry.

The second group went to the dockyard. While these men had to face the cold, damp northern air, they had ample opportunity to scavenge rice and beans from the broken bags they unloaded from the supply ships. They would tie their pant legs at the ankles and pour the rice straight down their pants. The trick was not to get too greedy and come off the dock looking like a stuffed toy.

The final group were the truly unlucky. They were assigned to the coal yard, where they would spend fourteen-hour days outside pushing around loaded coal cars with their bare hands and feet. There were no safety rails on the tracks, so if they slipped they'd fall to certain death in the water below.

Ralph had not been assigned to any work group. He was too weak to walk. Afraid that he'd be bayoneted on the spot, he tried to stand, but his legs buckled under him. He had lost half of his body mass. His bones jutted out of his skin like bamboo shoots. His face was gaunt. He was, again, very near death. He was taken away from the courtyard to the infirmary on a stretcher and left there.

A guard approached Ralph and began to take his shoes off. Ralph protested, kicking his feet about and telling him to stop. This angered the soldier. He pulled Ralph by the collar of his shirt and punched him square in the nose. Ralph's blood gushed onto both their chests. This made the soldier more furious.

"No work—no boots!"

Another punch was levelled.

Ralph spent his first night in Japan bloodied, shoeless, and immobilized.

Those who could not work were given less food. He was not in an infirmary. He was on death row.

Ralph would have died in that room but for another angel. This one did not come with a red cross. This was a living, breathing angel. This angel was from Welland, Ontario. His name was Henry Marsolais. For the next three months, every single night Henry would come back from his work detail, stand in line for his slop, and bring Ralph anything he could get his hands on. It was mostly rice gruel with a piece of leaf affectionately known as *green horror*. If he was lucky, he might get a thumbnail-size piece of fish. It would have had to be poison for Ralph not to eat it.

By November Ralph was able to walk again, albeit slowly. The Canadian commanding officers knew he would still not last a day on a work detail. One of them remembered Ralph had been in charge of the liquor chest in Gander, Newfoundland. They knew that the Japanese camp commandant was a heavy drinker. He and his senior officers needed someone to help with menial tasks around their quarters. Ralph could be trusted to keep his head down and not do anything stupid.

His first act of labour in Japan was to take a plate full of steamed fish and shaved *daikon* to Commandant Tetsutaro Kato. Commandant Kato, or "four eyes," as the Canadians would refer to him, was infamous for his callous cruelty. He had ordered and committed some terrible acts. A few days after Ralph started his duties, two men, an American and a Canadian, were caught committing some misdemeanor. As punishment, both were stripped down to their undershirts and trousers and tied to a stake hammered into the frozen ground. In order to stay alive, they were forced to jog around the stake for the entire night. The other men lay helplessly in their hut listening to their comrades grunt and groan. At dawn, they awoke to the terrible sound of rifle butts beating the men. The American's body was left at the stake. His head was split open and pieces of his brain had frozen to the ground.

Miraculously, Mortimer survived both the night and the dawn beating. But his frostbitten body became ravaged by gangrene. His flesh rotted and for weeks he suffered in unspeakable agony as the decomposition continued its relentless march. He literally died from the toes up.

This episode solidified Commandant Kato's standing in the eyes of every man on the camp. He was a monster.

But Ralph came to know that he was also a learned man. Born into an influential Tokyo family, Kato had gone to university and socialized with scholars, business leaders, and politicians. He had a bright future ahead of him. Then he was commissioned into the army and sent to Manchuria. There, he started to drink heavily. He arrived in Niigata an angry drunkard.

The war had robbed Kato of many things, but not his curiosity. He called Ralph by his last name, which sounded like "Mac-u-rane." One night, Ralph had finished opening the second bottle of whisky for him and was about to return to the mess hall when Kato spoke softly, showing no sign of being intoxicated.

"Mac-u-rane. Wife?"

Ralph looked closely at Kato's face. He didn't want to speak, but an answer was expected.

"No," he said. He did not bow. He had forgotten. The slight went unnoticed or ignored.

"Mac-u-rane, drive car?"

This was by far the longest Ralph had ever spoken to a Japanese person. Kato also happened to be the highest-ranking Japanese person he'd ever come into contact with. He wanted to keep this short, tight, non-offensive.

"Yes, a truck. Back home."

"Ah, back a home." Kato looked past Ralph. He didn't say anything else, just nodded and seemed to be lost in thought. Maybe he was thinking about his home, maybe he was imagining Ralph's. Either way, Ralph saw an exit and took it. As he slid the door shut behind him, he saw Kato in the dim light of his hut, smoke from his pipe filling the room. He was still nodding and repeating the word *home*.

Both of them were so very far away from it.

On the night of December 31, 1944, a heavy snowfall was not able dampen the men's New Year's Eve celebration. Those in Ralph's hut scraped together the few cigarettes they had and passed them around. Ralph rolled away from them, hoping that 1945 would bring an end to all of this. It turned out to be a classic case of being careful what you wish for.

Each sleeping hut housed one hundred and eighty men. The huts were built of wood and had a dirt floor. They had been hastily set up. The Japanese had not anticipated capturing prisoners, let alone bringing them to Japan. Nor had they anticipated the record snowfalls that year. The hut roofs were lined with heavy tiles. Two levels of sleeping planks, seven feet long, were attached to opposite walls. The top bunks were five feet above the lower ones. Each man had a rice-straw mat for bedding. Ralph's hut had a pesky hole in the roof where one of the heavy tiles had blown off a few nights earlier, allowing the wind to howl through. Everyone felt sorry for the poor chap who slept below the hole, but nobody offered to switch places.

The hut's night watchman was finishing his rounds. He was just entering Ralph's hut to return to his bunk when he heard a loud *crack*. It sounded like a baseball bat knocking a hardball out of the park. The wood was moving, bending. As the watchman stared from the threshold, the doorway shifted sideways as the entire building collapsed under the weight of the snow.

Ralph awoke to someone or something hitting him on the shoulder. He thought it was a guard pounding him with one of those despised clubs. One of the two-foot ceiling beams had slammed into his shoulder, missing his skull by an inch and knocking him off his platform to the dirt floor. Amazingly unharmed, he stood up. He rubbed the dust out of his eyes and looked up; he saw a sky full of stars and felt heavy snow falling on his face. He looked down and saw the roof of the hut spread out around him. He was standing in the gap left by the missing tile. Men inches to the left and right of him had been crushed. He heard the cries of injured and dying men around him and registered the gravity of the situation. One hundred and seventy-eight men were trapped. The night watchman was already running to alert everyone. Ralph stood exactly where he was.

Other POWs ran to the scene and desperately tried to dig through the rubble with their bare hands. They were pulling men out when the guards' whistles stopped all efforts. Worried about men escaping, they wanted to count the prisoners. All rescue ceased as the men lined up in the parade square, helplessly staring at the pile of wood and snow. They knew that as they stood there being counted off, their buried friends were dying. Tears ran down their cheeks.

Ralph would think later that it was ironic. Of all the things that had taken him to the edge—bullets, mortars, bayonets, diphtheria, the hellship journey—of all these things, it was snow that had come closest to sending this Canadian boy to his grave.

Eight men died that night under the rubble, three-and-a-half hours into the new year, their third in captivity.

If only that had been the final degradation. The bodies had frozen, and in order to fit them into the Japanese caskets, the living were forced to break the bodies. Legs, ribs, and pelvises were snapped, folded, and jammed into the wooden boxes. The men left alive lost a part of themselves that morning as they lowered the eight broken bodies into the frozen ground.

CHAPTER 7

Mitsue's War

Mitsue and Hideo had to report to the Canadian Pacific Railway Station at 8 a.m. sharp. Mitsue was up before dawn. She had been awake the entire night. She ran a bath and put on her best skirt and blouse. She had ironed them both the night before. She put on a little makeup.

Mitsue had never heard the house so quiet. She tiptoed down the stairs, made a cup of tea, and sat at the table by herself. She was preparing herself, trying to brace herself, gather her strength. She knew she'd need it.

Hanpei and Wari came down the stairs together. Mitsue made more tea and some somen noodles for them.

"*Arigato,*" they said.

It was a day like no other. Their trunks were packed, nailed, and stacked by the front door.

Mitsue made a little *nigiri* for Hideo and June and then cleaned the dishes. When they were both done eating, Mitsue put the bowls and chopsticks into the basket that would be left for the rooming house owner. What use were they to them anymore?

They left the kitchen together. Hideo turned out the light and they waited in the front lobby in the half-light of dawn. Not a word was spoken. Mitsue was glad that she had taken a little time to prepare herself because she felt a wave of emotion. She swallowed hard to keep it at bay; to keep it all inside. She was so frightened to leave.

The truck they had arranged arrived right at 7 a.m. The outfit had taken many Japanese families to the train station, so the driver knew how to handle the wooden boxes. He stacked them quickly and neatly in the back of the truck. As they drove away, Mitsue didn't turn around to watch the boarding house or Little Tokyo fade away. She kept her eyes forward and tried not to blink. She didn't want tears ruining her makeup. She kept her hands folded in her lap so nobody would notice them shaking. Amid the confusion, terror, and anxiety, there was an unspoken code of silence. Everyone's hands were folded. Everyone's hands were shaking. They tried to be Japanese in the best way they knew how, by keeping their composure, keeping their civility.

Mitsue met her family on the train station platform. They were all dressed in their Sunday clothes too. Yosuke had his overcoat on even though the sun was starting to warm the air and the grey morning mist was lifting. They had packed less than Mitsue had. It looked like they were going on a camping trip. Susanne had made sure to bring all of her school books, even though nobody knew if she'd be able to find a school where they were going. Mary had a deck of cards and a few board games to pass the time. She had a Ouija board too. Maybe she would look for some answers there. Where were they going? What would it be like? Why was this happening?

The station was full of Japanese folks. Mitsue looked across the platform. Half of them were children. Some she knew from Sunday school.

They had to load their own trunks on the train. Pat and Hideo did most of the heavy lifting for the two families. Once that was done, an officer with a bullhorn ordered everyone to board.

Mitsue felt like a cow at Hastings Park. Her heart sank as she sat down on a wooden bench. Her worst fears were coming true. She sat by the window and Hideo sat next to her. He took her arm as the train jerked forward. Clickety-clack down the tracks, the train made them sway back and forth in their seats. Mitsue saw a policeman standing on a box with a rifle, staring at the train as it went by. His face was blank. There were some people on the platform still holding hands through the windows with loved ones on the train, and running alongside it. They didn't want to say goodbye. One man panicked. He wouldn't let go of his wife's hand. Finally, as the train picked up speed, he fell onto the platform. His whole family was gone. His wife was sitting with two small children a few rows up from Mitsue. She put her hands to her face and cried until she fell asleep.

The train left the station at 8:45 a.m. They were in a dirty old car with rows of wooden benches. It smelt of dust and sweat and dirt. There were no dining cars or food of any kind. There was one common toilet and it hadn't been cleaned in some time. Passengers and luggage were all packed in tight. A lady a few rows back complained loudly that they were being treated like pigs. She was speaking in loud Japanese and then burst into tears.

The scenery outside was familiar but already everything felt different. Mitsue was saying goodbye to the city of Vancouver, goodbye to her life as she knew it. It had been taken away from her—all of it. The Sunday school kids, her job with Mrs. Yamamoto, sunny afternoons in Stanley Park with friends, family dinners in Celtic, the thrill of starting her own life. This city was throwing her out. She and every single person she loved had been uprooted and discarded.

By evening, they were at the foot of the Rocky Mountains. Mitsue had never seen them before. She thought they were beautiful. They looked like a great wall. The passengers had no idea what was on the other side of the mountains. The train slowed to start the steep climb. Mitsue wondered if they were too heavy to make it.

Night fell and the world became full of shadows. The moon hid behind the clouds. It was the most restless of nights. Mitsue could not lie down anywhere, so she leaned on Hideo. The metal sides of the train were cold going through the mountains. Everyone kept their jackets zipped tight.

As day broke, they found themselves east of the Rockies, making their way through the foothills. Another world opened up before them. They had never seen anything like it; miles and miles of emptiness stretched as far as their sleepy eyes could see. There was a silence in the vastness. Mitsue felt as empty as the horizon.

Everyone ate some of the *onigiri* that Mitsue had packed for breakfast. She had known that the rice balls would travel well and be appreciated. She passed them out to Hideo, June, Hanpei, and Wari. You seldom know exactly what someone is thinking, but when sharing food, you know just what the person is experiencing. They ate in silence.

As the morning wore on, people talked more. Mitsue visited with her Celtic neighbours. They hadn't been told much, but they did know that each family would disperse as soon as the train stopped. They all feared they would not see one another again for a long, long time.

After lunch, everyone was tired. Most dozed off. Those who did awoke sometime later with a jerk that sent many flying out of their seats. Groggy, Mitsue tumbled down the steps, blinked to see daylight, and stretched her cramped body.

Where were they? It was like waking up from a bad dream.

They were at the train station in Lethbridge, Alberta, just east of the Rocky Mountains and in the Canadian prairies. Each family disembarked and assembled their belongings, staying together until their name was announced and the family was matched with a farmer who had contracted to use them as labourers on sugar beet farms. Mitsue stood with her family as tall and as straight as she could in her Sunday best as men walked past her, staring at her, claiming her with their eyes.

On the train, she had been a prisoner. Off the train, she was a slave.

A farmer by the name of Oscar Johnson took her parents, Mary,

Susanne, and Pat. He was a large Swedish man in overalls with a round face and ruddy cheeks. He told them they were going to his farm in Coaldale, ten miles outside Lethbridge.

Soon after that, a farmer with a wide gait slowly made his way towards Mitsue. He was staring back and forth between her and the paper he held in his hand.

"Youse Sakamatos?"

"Sakamoto family," Hideo said, waving his finger to indicate them.

"Okay. I'm Mr. Rutt, and you are all coming to work for me."

Hideo nodded and picked up the rice box. He nodded to everyone else to do likewise.

That was it. They had all been claimed and would soon be on their way to their new homes. They were given ten minutes to write down where their friends and family were going. They all ran around exchanging P.O. box numbers on scraps of paper.

Where are you going?

Barnwell.

Where are you going?

Taber.

Where are you going?

Raymond. It is south of here.

Where are you going?

Picture Butte. It's across a ravine, only it's dry so they call them coulees.

They were loaded onto the backs of farmers' trucks and transported to these unknown destinations with only the clothes on their backs and their bags. Mitsue, Hideo, Hanpei, Wari, and June all bounced around in the back of Rutt's big old truck. It was full of manure. She tried to hang on and not fall into it.

The last few miles were bumpy and Wari was still very sore on her left side. It was a lingering pain from a fall in Vancouver. Hideo tried to keep her still. The truck took a sharp left onto a laneway and Mitsue could see a big barn and an old farmhouse. It was a desolate-looking place. Rutt hit the brakes hard, jolting everyone forward, and they stopped with a thud. Wari moaned.

Mitsue's teeth were clenched from stress as they gathered them-selves slowly. Hideo was off first and he helped everyone down from the truck. The ground was muddy and Mitsue's heels sank. She felt silly for having worn those shoes, but she had wanted to make a good impression on the people whose custody they would be in. She wanted them to know that her family were decent and civilized. That they were not enemies, they were not animals.

"Your place is behind the barn. Unload your stuff and I'll come by to show you around."

They each picked up a bag and made their way towards the barn. Mitsue stepped carefully around the muddy patches. The dirt path was only a hundred yards or so, but it was the longest walk of her life. Mitsue's body became more tense with each step. She hoped that the house behind the barn would be decent. The barn itself was not a good omen. It was a rickety thing that needed paint. Through the wooden slates she could see a few horses moving around.

They had to follow a trail along the side of the barn. Hideo was leading the way, so he saw the place before anyone else. Mitsue was ten paces back. She noticed a few wild prairie flowers growing alongside the barn before looking up to see Hideo stop suddenly, looking straight ahead.

Mitsue tightened her grip on her bag and took her last ten paces with dread. As she stood beside Hideo, she saw a chicken coop. There were no chickens in it. Attached to it was an old shack. It looked like an outhouse, only bigger. There were no walls or win-dows, just wooden slats nailed together. As with the barn, you could see through them. The roof was made of planks as well. The hut was surrounded by mud and prairie wild grass. She thought that the grass in front might be a pasture because of the cow droppings.

Mitsue stood beside Hideo in shock. Nobody said a word. They just stared at the old shack. Wari set her bag down on a dry patch of grass. Nobody wanted to open the front door. They stood there for some time. Finally Mr. Rutt came out of his house and opened the shack door for them.

Mitsue ducked her head to avoid a big cobweb and took her first step in. There was a dirt floor. There was one bed in the corner of the room and a small wood stove beside a decrepit wooden table held together by rusted nails. Everything was filthy. Everywhere they looked they could see outside through the gaps in the walls. The wind whistled right through the shack.

What were they supposed to do with the place?

Mr. Rutt was apologetic. He explained that he had cleared out the chickens and patched up the roof so the rain wouldn't get in. The shack had only been used in the summer months for migrant workers. It had never needed to be insulated. He promised he'd get to it before winter came around.

Before winter? Mitsue couldn't think about staying here for one more minute. She wanted to run.

Mr. Rutt said he hadn't realized that there would be five in the family. He said that he would bring another bed that could sleep Hideo and Mitsue. June would have to sleep with Hanpei and Wari. Mitsue looked around again and realized that they would all be sleeping, cooking, and eating in the one room. Her ears were ringing, her heart pounding. Mr. Rutt left to get the bed and closed the door behind him.

They stood there in silence, the women in their Sunday dresses, purses in hand, the men in their coats and hats. They didn't know where to begin. They could hear and feel the wind blow through the shack. The sunlight came in through the cracks in the walls. In the stillness, they watched the dust floating in the air around them. Dirt, dust, grime, wind. They were in Alberta. They were home.

Shikata-ga-nai. They got on with it.

First things first. June and Mitsue changed out of their shoes so that they could help unload the boxes from the truck.

Their water source was a dugout one mile to the west of the shack. The water had to be boiled because the cows and horses drank from it, walked in it, and excreted into it. Mr. Rutt gave Hideo a few pails to cart up to the farmhouse hose to fetch drinking water.

Rutt returned with another bed, a single.

That night Mitsue lay as still as she could. Hanpei was snoring. She tried not to shake and wake up Hideo. But she had to let it out. It just had to come out. She cried all night long.

The next morning, Hideo was up first. He had already lit a fire and was making tea they had brought from Vancouver. The familiar smell made everyone feel a little better. Mitsue wondered if her parents were faring any better. She went to the dugout and got some water for washing. Scooping it up from the muddy bank, she examined the pail, picking out a few leaves. The water was dirty brown.

Walking back into the shack, she saw Hideo inspecting June's back. There were red marks all over her. Hanpei was just getting out of the bed and undoing his *yukata*. His shoulder was covered with red marks too. Wari—still sore—stayed in the bed. Mitsue walked over to her and saw red marks on her neck. They'd never seen bedbug bites before. Hideo and Hanpei took their mattress outside, leaned it against the side of the shack, and beat it with sticks to try to get the bugs out. It didn't do any good.

Those first few weeks, they were scavengers, looking for everything and anything: food, utensils, furniture, a mirror, coffee cups, and coffee beans. By the second week, they had completely run out of the food they had brought, except for the tinned box of white rice. They still had plenty of that. Slowly, they accumulated what they needed, mostly from scraps that they got from Mr. Rutt.

They also started to work.

Rutt had about ten acres directly behind the shack. The west side of his land was lined with big poplar trees and long grass. It was empty, just earth and sky. For about half an hour Mr. Rutt showed them how to work the land. It all seemed simple enough. Everyone grabbed a hoe and started from the northwest corner. They had two days to seed the whole field.

On Mitsue's first day of manual labour she felt like a sentenced prisoner. The sun beat down on her and the hoe soon became heavy and burned her hands. By the third hour, everyone except Hideo was exhausted. Wari was very weak—her side was still hurting. Hanpei could still work but he was an old man. June was only fourteen, her frame too weak for such labour. Hideo picked up everyone's slack.

The sun was relentless. They took turns walking to the far end of the field to sit for a few minutes underneath the trees. The mosquitoes attacked. Dust packed their nostrils, dirt got entangled in their hair, grime jammed into their fingernails. Their throats were dry, their hands were welted, their backs ached.

But Mitsue didn't complain.

That night they ate rice with a little chicken they got from Mr. Rutt. Everyone collapsed in bed after the dishes were done. Mitsue fell asleep dreaming of bedbugs crawling over her.

Every day after that was just like the last. They were suspended in a dustbowl of a terrible dream. There was no waking from it.

As the spring days turned to summer, the sun became their primary torturer. They'd wrap up in scarves to block it. That made them hotter, but it prevented sunstroke. That was the most important thing—sunstroke would keep you out of the field for at least a day. That cost money, money they needed. A bag of rice was five dollars, so they'd all work from dawn to dusk for a bag of rice. It was survival. Every single cent gave them life. Not a nice life, just life. They all had to survive this ordeal.

The work was backbreaking. As summer wore on, the days got longer and hotter. There wasn't a cloud in the prairie sky. The temperature rose to forty degrees. They were paid by the beet weight, not the hour, so they always had to be on the go. They only stopped for water. Even then, Mitsue would have to call hard-working Hideo in from the field at the end of the day. She'd often have to yell to make him hear her, he was concentrating so hard on what he was doing and, as he always did when he was working, he whispered her name over and over, as if to soothe himself: "Mits . . . Mits . . . Mits . . . Mits . . ."

Those summer days hit Wari hard. Her left side just kept getting worse. There was no doctor in Coaldale, so she and Mitsue had to take a day off and go to Lethbridge in Mr. Rutt's truck. Nobody had an Alberta licence, so a farmhand had to drive them. Lethbridge had banned Japanese people within the city limits, so before they could get to a doctor, Hideo had to go to City Hall and obtain a special permit.

Wari and Mitsue left with the farmhand early one morning. The old truck had bad shocks and it was a very rough ride. Wari moaned all the way. Every bump was a fresh blow. When they pulled up to the hospital, the farmhand seemed glad to see them leave. Mitsue escorted Wari to the front desk, where they waited for a long time. A dozen people went through before them. Finally, a nurse came out and called them in. It was Mitsue's second time in a hospital. The Lethbridge hospital was much smaller than the one in Vancouver where Toru had passed away.

The doctor walked in with his nose in a chart.

"Name?"

Mitsue spoke for her mother-in-law

He looked at Mitsue.

"What's the problem?"

"She has a very sore left side. We are not sure why."

"Okay, I'll give her something for that."

And that was it. He didn't even touch her, just wrote something on his prescription pad, handed it to Mitsue, and was out the door.

They got the medicine. Mitsue dropped off Wari in their shack and went back to the fields.

That very night, Mitsue was staying up a little later to read when Wari sat straight up from a dead sleep. Mitsue turned up the kerosene lamp. Wari sat as straight as a board. She didn't move her head, she looked straight ahead. Her eyes were wide open. After a moment, she slumped back down without saying a word; she was gone. She was only forty-nine years old, but her body could not take the conditions. Her heart had given out.

Mitsue woke everyone up and they all said goodbye to Wari in the cold of the night. They buried her the next day in a small grave-yard just down the road from the shack. The wooden headstone was the only one with Japanese writing on it.

They went back to work that afternoon. They were to weed that day. Mitsue cried as she picked at the earth. Hanpei spent much of the day leaning on his hoe, shivering and shaking. June went to get water more often than usual, to cry in private. But Hideo worked all afternoon. He worked harder that day than Mitsue had ever seen him work before. The harder he worked, the less likely it was that Wari's fate would befall anyone else in his family.

If Wari's death was an ending, the shack saw a beginning too. Mitsue was pregnant. She was surprised that she felt thrilled. Despite all the hardship there was one constant: family was the most important thing. *Because* of the hardship, family was the most important thing.

Mitsue wasn't a branch anymore. She was becoming part of the trunk. She had to be steady and sturdy. It was her time to support the branches. It would be tough. They didn't even have running water. There were still holes in the walls. Bugs could fly right in. The shack was no place to raise a baby. But she had to live her life. The tree had to grow. In spite of it all, everyone had to grow.

Mitsue spent the next three months hoeing and throwing up. Life couldn't stop because she was pregnant. The family needed the money she made, so every day, even on the worst days, she was out in the hot, dusty field, thirsty and sick to her stomach. Those were the hardest days of Mitsue's life. Despite it all, she was excited to know she would soon have a baby of her own. She knew that despite everything that was happening around her, she could be a good mother.

Mitsue knew she needed some light in her life. Just like teach-ing Bible stories to the children of Celtic had helped her through Toru's death, she decided, showing a baby love and warmth would bring those things into her own life. The shack was always so quiet. Everyone was bone-tired, morning and night. They spoke in orders. *Do this. Take that over there.* It felt more like a work camp than a family. Mitsue thought a baby might change that. Maybe being close to new life would remind them all just what life was supposed to be. Mostly she hoped having a baby would make their condition more bearable. But for the next few months, it just made her existence even harder.

Fall was coming and that meant they had to start to harvest. They had to pull each beet out of the ground by hand, shake all of the earth off, cut off the top and the roots at the bottom, and put it in a pile. The piles of beets would get to be six feet high.

It seemed the rows of sugar beets would never end. They had to hurry. They only had so much time to get those vegetables out of the ground before the frost came. If the beets weren't picked, they wouldn't get paid. If they weren't paid, they'd starve.

They got the beets out just in time. Winter came fast and hard. The heat and the mosquitoes had been terrible, but they were nothing compared to the cold. They had not known cold like that. It hardly snowed on the coast. Here, the first flurry was light, like big pieces of salt coming down. But by the next morning, the ground was covered. The table was wet because snow had fallen through the cracks in the roof. They knew that they couldn't keep living in the shack for much longer or they'd freeze to death.

Mr. Rutt brought in a carpenter to patch up all the holes and insulate where he could. This was better, but still pretty rough. The nails in the wood would frost over every morning. Ice filled the cracks in the walls. During those winter nights, they would all sleep with one eye open. If the fire in the stove went out, they'd be in big trouble. When it is minus 35 degrees outside, you don't have much time once the fire goes out.

Hideo went up to the farmhouse to speak to Mr. Rutt about the conditions. He had never complained, not about the bedbugs, not about the dirty grey water, not even about the holes in the walls. But the cold was dangerous. They could die out there in that exposed little shack. There were only a few boards of wood between his family and the cold, hard prairie wind.

Mr. Rutt just said, "That's the best I can do."

They had to move. They were bringing a baby into the world and the shack was not fit for it. But they had no money to move. The harvest was over and Mr. Rutt only had ten acres, so they hadn't made much. Certainly not enough to move—not even enough to make it through the winter months. With twenty-four dollars for five months, they were destitute.

Mitsue went out looking for winter work and found a small job mending dresses in Coaldale. It was nice to be back in a warm shop working with a sewing machine. The first few days were difficult because her hands were so calloused she had difficulty threading the needle and delicately guiding the cloth through the machine. It reminded her of her work in Vancouver, of better days. But now her hands looked like those of a beggar, cracked, with caked-in dirt. It didn't matter how hard she scrubbed them, they were stained with hard work.

Hideo and Hanpei took up work at a large farm. A truck picked them up every morning at seven. This gave them an extra hour of sleep. Waking up each morning was a hardship. The bedpan would be frozen. They had to run outside to do their ablutions.

Mitsue's morning sickness subsided, but she was getting bigger. As she grew over that winter, everyone agreed that they had to move from the Rutt farm. There was no choice. The shack was just too cold. Rutt's land was too small.

By mid-winter they were flat broke. Winter work was tough to come by, maybe an odd job here and there for Hideo, but that wasn't enough to keep the family going. Huddled in the old shack, they could hear—and feel—the cold prairie wind sweep across the barren white land. They were alone, isolated, and totally lost. They had been brought out to work with the sugar beets and that was all done. Now what? Nobody had an answer. They were just sitting here like squatters. They had to break the ice in the dugout and melt it for water. They had no money, no prospects, no food.

Everyone felt numb, except for Hideo. He just said, *Let's find another farm and get different jobs for the winter*. That was that. He cleaned himself up, put on some slacks, and went to Mr. Rutt's front door and knocked. June, Hanpei, and Mitsue watched from the shack. They could see him smiling at Mr. Rutt, smiling and shaking his head. He was thanking him. Actually thanking him. And apologizing. He said he was sorry that his family could not continue working his land, but it was not enough to sustain them, and with a baby on the way they needed more work. They needed more money. He thanked him for fixing the shack up. They shook hands.

Hideo turned and walked back. They were all standing there at the table staring at him.

"That's it," he said.

They ate the last of the rice from the tinned box that evening. Mitsue's cup scraped the bottom as she reached for each grain. Over dinner, Hideo said that he thought they could get on at a farm close to the one where Mitsue's parents worked, a few miles down the highway. He would go there tomorrow. He was decisive. Mitsue's shoulders straightened a little that day. In her mind's eye she kept seeing Hideo smiling at Mr. Rutt. She loved him for it. That man knew how to smile.

The next morning, Hideo dressed in his warmest clothes and walked the three and a half miles to the farm he had mentioned the night before. He caught the owner just as he was pulling his truck out of the lane. He agreed to take them on provided they clean up the vacant farmhouse in the back. It was a real trade up. The house was vacant and dirty, but it had actual walls and no animals had lived in it.

Mitsue's first child, Ronald Satoshi, would be born into a home.

Before Ron could walk, Mitsue was pregnant again. She had just gone back to work sewing, so she tried to conceal the pregnancy for as long as she could. She'd wrap her clothes tight like an obi around her waist. She ended up working right up until the very day Glory was born.

Mitsue had to be out in the field as soon as she could walk around—three days after Glory was born. It was midway through their second harvest. Running between the field and the farmhouse, Mitsue spent her days not knowing if she was coming or going.

When Glory got a little bigger, she could be taken outside while the adults worked. Hideo would haul out a little table and set up Glory's baby dolls. The children had a chalkboard for writing on and Ron had a few toy trucks. Hideo bought him a little string guitar that he would play all the time. They grew up along the treeline of the farm, playing in the shade as their family laboured.

Come lunchtime, Mitsue would gather her children and take them indoors to eat. She'd take them back after lunch and get them set up again. Ron would always ask, "Can you stay with us, Momma? Just for a bit?" She never could.

The adults put on their overalls and went out into the field every day. They would come back dirty and callused, their backs bent, their fingers cut up. Dirt found its way everywhere: into their mouths and hair. That was their life. Hideo and Mitsue had not been on a date, had not had a single meal out since their wedding night. They worked and slept.

By the winter of 1943, it was clear that they were not going to be heading home anytime soon. They had thought they would be allowed back to B.C. by Christmas. It was dawning on Mitsue that her family could be out on that field for years. The more she yearned to return, the further away it seemed.

Meanwhile, their world in Vancouver was disappearing. The politicians in B.C. had employed a scorched earth policy. They didn't want the Japanese to come back and they were doing their best to make sure they wouldn't.

Mitsue hardly ever got mail. Who was there to write to? What was there to say? When a letter from her friend in Celtic was delivered to the main farm house, her heart sang. In her memory, she traced where the envelope she held had been. The stamp might have been purchased at the Shintanis' confectionery store down the street from her beloved row house. Mitsue hurried indoors, desperate to read the letter.

She opened the envelope slowly, savouring the mundane, everyday task. She slid the neatly folded paper out of the envelope and opened it up. Mitsue knew that the letter had been opened and inspected by the censors. There were no black marks on it, but there was not much to censor. The letter was only a few sentences long.

The Cultural Centre in Celtic had burned down. It was gone. Everything in it was ashes.

Burned down? Who would do such a thing? They had stored their life memories in that building: family photo albums, religious shrines, precious kimonos, family heirlooms from Japan passed down from generation to generation.

Mitsue had never felt so alone. Her home was very far away. Was it even home anymore? All of their family possessions were gone, either confiscated, stolen, or burned. The fire sent a message: *Don't come back. You are not wanted here.*

Mitsue was glad that nobody was home. She would have tried to keep it all in. She would have tried to maintain her composure. Sitting there alone, she let the tears come. They soaked the letter lying on the table. She said goodbye to her life in Vancouver. This situation was not temporary. This shabby farm might be their new life. The thought made her cry even harder. It was such a hard life. She didn't want to live like this. She couldn't let her children live like this.

She had to tell her parents. She picked herself up from the table, dried her eyes, put on a little makeup to cover the puffiness, and made her way to her parents' house. She walked in the ditch most of the way, afraid that gravel would flick up and hit her if a truck drove past. She paused at the laneway entrance. She could see Yosuke working on a piece of farm equipment. She wanted to just keep walking. Yosuke looked up, saw Mitsue, and waved. He was smiling as she walked up the lane. Mitsue hugged him and asked if her mother was around.

"In the house. What is wrong, Mitsue?" he asked. Her face had given her away.

They went into the house and sat down in the kitchen. Mitsue began to explain, but the words escaped her. She sat there staring at her parents.

"The Centre was burned down. They burned it right to the ground." She bowed her head. Tears fell onto her folded hands.

Her parents did not cry. They did not even flinch.

"Don't cry, Mitsue, we have each other. They can't burn that down. We have our dignity. That can't be turned to ashes."

Tomi passed Mitsue a handkerchief. "It was just things. Not life."

They quietly finished their cup of *ocha* and then Mitsue walked home. This time she stayed on the road.

PART 3

Release

Going Home

With the war winding down, anti-Asian groups looked to solid-ify their gains. They had had the Japanese removed. Now, they wanted them gone for good. One hundred miles was not enough. They wanted an ocean between the Japanese and B.C.'s jobs. In Prime Minister King, they found a sympathetic ear. King knew he needed to carry the B.C. seats in the upcoming spring 1945 election. He cut a deal. He would give the Japanese Canadians a choice: go east of the Rockies after the war, or go back to Japan. By 1944, nearly half the Japanese—over ten thousand—were facing government repatriation.

Mitsue could hardly look at a newspaper. She stopped taking Ron to the grocery store. One by one, each provincial premier came out against allowing Japanese to remain in their province after the war: Alberta, Quebec, Ontario, Manitoba . . . each garnering his own headline.

Time magazine ran a cover with the headline WHO WANTS JAPS? No TAKERS.

Mayors, premiers, the prime minister—all had a message for the Japanese of Canada: Go home.

The problem was, they *were* home.

A mother is the most desperate person. Mitsue could not do anything to protect her children. It ate at her day and night. She continued to toil in the fields daily. At every break, Mitsue would rush over to Ron and Glory playing in the shade. She wondered if life would be worse as war refugees in Japan.

Their turn came. The dreaded letter from the Department of Labour arrived. Mitsue hated to see anything that looked official. It was always bad news. Everyone gathered around Hideo as he slowly opened the envelope. The stamp was four cents and it had a picture of a soldier on it. The letter said that the government would pay for them to go to Japan after the war—or sooner if that could be arranged.

The Canadian government was paying its citizens to leave. It was a bribe of the worst kind. Some people agreed to go. They were terrified of being separated from their families or being left homeless. Nobody knew what might happen. They signed in fear.

There would be no signature from Mitsue and Hideo. The letter was neatly folded and put back in the envelope. It was stored with the other government documents. Mitsue's heart swelled. They were Canadians. They were not going to agree to go anywhere. They had—for the time being—made a decision about their fate. They had said no. It felt good to stand their ground. But it came with consequences. The letter had ended with a terrifyingly banal threat:

These assurances do not apply to persons of the Japanese race repatriated on other than a voluntary basis.

There was no reading between the lines. Agree to go now and we'll pay for your trip. If we kick you out later, you're on your own.

A few weeks later, on August 6, 1945, at thirty thousand feet above Hiroshima, Japan, a much less banal event occurred.

William Parsons's nickname was Deak. He was the chief of the Ordinance Division for the Manhattan Project. He knew "Little

Boy" better than anyone, so the job fell on him to arm the world's first atomic bomb en route to the target. It took him fifteen minutes.

The sky was clear at 3:02 a.m. As the bomb doors opened, Deak saw below him a city.

Three minutes later, 70,000 lives were lost, their shadows imposed against melted walls. They may have been the lucky ones. The fate of the living was indescribable—their faces simply melted. It was impossible to tell if you were looking at the front or the back of a person—unless you could spot a mouth.

Another 70,000 would die. One bomb, 140,000 souls.

September 2, 1945, marked the war's end for most of the world. For Mitsue, things went on exactly the same. Nothing changed. They were not free to go. They had no money to go anywhere even if the end of the war had brought them freedom.

After concluding the war with Japan, the Canadian government turned its mind to the Japanese problem at home. Prime Minister King passed three orders-in-council which, together, laid the legal foundation for mass deportation. All told, 10,347 Japanese were on the deportation list, three-quarters of them Canadian-born citizens. Thousands were children. The prime minister hastily wrote General Douglas MacArthur, stating that his government was "anxious to proceed with the repatriation and deportation as soon as this can be arranged without causing you embarrassment. . . . You will appreciate the desire of the Canadian Government to proceed with these plans as soon as possible. The Canadian Government would be grateful for your advice as to the earliest date on which you would be prepared to have these people arrive in Japan."

But perhaps the veneer of national security had worn thin with the cessation of hostilities. Whatever the reason, Japanese Canadians finally began receiving some support from their fellow Canadians. It couldn't have come at a better time.

By December 27, 1945, enough funds had been raised by

Japanese Canadians and other concerned Canadians to retain counsel and issue writs against Attorney General St. Laurent to test the validity of the deportation in a court of law. Astonishingly, this was the first legal action ever taken to protest the years of injustice. Citizens took to the streets and held vigils. Over one thousand people crammed into Toronto's Jarvis Collegiate Institute to hear Rabbi Abraham Feinberg speak up. He knew only too well what happened when silence prevailed.

"I am here on behalf of six million Jews who were slaughtered . . . for no reason other than being Jews. . . . The ghost of Hitler still walks in Canada. The thing for which Hitler stood has been inscribed on the order-in-council which punishes little children for crimes they couldn't commit."

The case was heard over two dark and miserable days in January 1946. Canada had yet to adopt the Bill of Rights. The lawyers had only technical arguments. There was no legal way to challenge the justice of the act itself.

They threw a Hail Mary legal argument. It struck at the most basic of legal principles: *habeas corpus*. To banish a citizen for any reason other than conviction of a legal offence debases the most fundamental principle underpinning our society: innocence until guilt has been proven. To deport based on grounds of ethnicity was a crime against humanity. Full stop.

The government lawyers had a much easier case to make. They simply needed to convince the court that the government was within its legal purview to enact the deportation orders. The government lawyers argued that the peace, order, and good government clause of the *British North America Act* gave the federal government full authority to pass the *War Measures Act* and the subsequent *Transitional Powers Act*. Because these acts were legitimate, all attached orders-in-council were to be adhered to and the content of those orders could not be examined by any court.

Without the Charter of Rights, the hands of the highest court in the land were tied. On February 20, 1946, the court ruled in favour of King's deportation orders, and the deportation machine heaved into motion. Japanese Canadians still on Canadian soil received gut-wrenching letters from deportees. They had arrived in a devastated country to work in a devastated economy among a devastated people that treated them as the enemy.

The expulsion process went on for a year, during which more than four thousand people were sent back to Japan. Prime Minister King finally repealed the deportation orders.

There was a collective sigh of relief from those who had avoided deportation. With their future secure in Canada, Japanese Canadians turned their minds to their property. So, too, did the government.

Mitsue and her family were free to leave Taber. But where to go? They had no money. They could barely buy food. For Mitsue, the war went on day after day. She wanted to return to Celtic. She longed for the ocean, the parks, the picnics. The life she had led seemed a distant dream. So much had been taken. There was about to be more.

Hanpei got another letter in the mail. It was from the Japanese Property Claims Commission. They were demanding that he go to the courthouse in Lethbridge to show evidence of his claim for property that had been seized and sold. The letter included a form that had to be filled out identifying all the belongings the family had had to leave behind. They did what was asked. It took them the entire evening as they walked through their Vancouver home in their minds, room by room:

2 washstands – $4.50
1 sideboard, base and top – $10
10 cross-cut saws – $100 . . .

It took the entire page to itemize their losses.

They finished and stared at the foolscap paper. It was their life, in material objects. They did the math. *You took our life as we knew it. Please repay us $818.*

Hanpei spent the week readying himself for court. On the appointed day, Mitsue fixed up a shirt and mended the nicest pair of trousers she could find. Hideo went with his father. They walked into the courthouse through the big oak front doors. The whole building seemed to be made of solid wood. It smelled of power.

Hanpei clutched his list. They sat in the chamber and waited their turn. They saw a few familiar faces, but nobody said anything to each other.

The court clerk called, "Hanpei Sakamoto."

Both men stood up. Hideo walked up to the bar with his father. They felt like they were on trial.

"Provide your list of chattels to the magistrate," stated the court clerk.

Hanpei handed it over.

"Is this everything?" the judge asked, perched high above them.

Hanpei nodded while keeping his head bowed. "That is everything we left—and a claim for lost wages."

"Hanpei Sakamoto, claiming eight hundred and one dollars and fifty cents in chattels and six hundred dollars in lost wages," stated the clerk.

"That is all," said the judge. "You may go."

With nothing more to add, Hanpei and Hideo both turned and left the courthouse. It was over in seconds.

Two months later, on August 5, 1947, another letter arrived from the government. The family was eagerly expecting the money. Mitsue dreamed of using it to finally get back to Vancouver, where she belonged. They could start their lives again. They could be free.

Hanpei's hands were shaking as he opened the envelope. Everyone gathered around the same table where they had made the list. Hanpei opened the letter, careful not to tear it. It was from the Department of the Secretary of State, Office of the Custodian, Japanese Evacuation Section. The letter was four sentences long.

Hanpei read it to himself and then put the paper down.

Mitsue picked it up and read it out loud.

Dear Sir:

Enclose herewith is Custodian cheque in the amount of $25.65.

These funds represent the net proceeds from sale of chattels as your property.

No funds remain to your credit with this office. No property identified as belonging to you remains under the control of the Custodian. Your account is therefore being closed.

Yours truly,

F. Matheson

There must be a mistake. Twenty-five dollars. My God.

Hanpei held the cheque. He looked at the back of it. He blinked twice. He too was looking for the error. He sat down and hung his head.

The next day he took the cheque and cashed it. They were too poor to be proud. It was not enough to get them to Vancouver, but it would buy food. They needed that.

Their file was closed. The government had washed its hands of the ordeal and they were on their own. They were free and they were trapped.

Hideo's friend Ted Nishimoto had taken agricultural schooling in Japan. He and his family lived down the road in Coaldale. Ted urged Hideo to think about moving his family to Medicine Hat. It had lots of sunshine, and tomatoes, cucumbers, and corn would grow well. The two men would speak late into the night.

Mitsue kept quiet, but after Ted left she let Hideo know what she thought. She did not want to move to Medicine Hat. It felt like surrender. She would be saying goodbye to Vancouver forever. She was not ready for that. Her mother and father, brother, and two sisters had already moved back to Vancouver. Yosuke had gotten some money for the two boats that had been confiscated. But Mitsue and Hideo didn't have enough to move back.

So, on November 5, 1948, they moved to Medicine Hat.

It had been six years, seven months, and twenty days since they stepped off the train from Vancouver to be claimed as labourers. In Medicine Hat they would still be labouring, but at least now it would be for themselves.

Mitsue and Hideo packed up their family and their few possessions. Mitsue put on her finest jacket—a full-length wool jacket with a fur collar. She dressed Ron is his best sweater, with images of two moose adorning the front. Glory was wrapped in a winter parka with white trim around the hood and collar.

Hanpei and Hideo were also dressed in their finest, topcoats and three-piece suits. Hideo wore a fedora, while Hanpei wore a fur trapper's hat. They had already packed what they needed in the cab of the Model T that they had bought from Pat after he left for Vancouver. He had sold it to them for a song. They piled in the car and sped away. There were no goodbyes. They were anxious to start the rest of their lives.

They had seventy-eight dollars between them, just enough to rent a small plot of land at the Golden Valley Farm two miles south of Medicine Hat. Hideo squinted as he turned onto the highway. The sun was rising. It was a new day.

But the new day didn't feel that much different from the day before, or the day before that.

It took two hours to reach the city limits of Medicine Hat, and another hour to find the small road that led to Golden Valley Farm. They drove ninety-four miles south under the great, open prairie sky. The farm was tucked away in a small coulee just west of the South Saskatchewan River. They cautiously pulled up to their new home. It looked much like their old home.

Mitsue wondered if it would ever end—the poverty, the struggle, the hopelessness.

As promised, the door was open. The house was quite dirty, but altogether livable. God knows, they had seen worse. They unpacked and began to clean their new house. Like everything else in their lives for the foreseeable future, it was rented.

But the land was good for farming. Ted Nishimoto said that it was well protected from the heavy prairie winds so not much topsoil would be lost.

The next morning, Hideo took the truck into town. He had a list of the basics Mitsue needed to clean the house and make dinner. He walked into the general store and saw a stack of newspapers. He read the headline. His knees weakened.

First Jap Family Moves to the Hat.

Such was their welcome.

CHAPTER 9

Mark 11:25

The day after Ralph escaped death by snow, he found the commandant unrepentant. The bandage on Ralph's left arm went unnoticed. Setting down a cup of green tea, the commandant was more interested in speaking to Ralph about the West. He always wanted to know about the West. He knew, to be sure, that the West would be victorious. That it was only a matter of time. There were rumours of a big bomb. He wanted to know what was coming for him.

"*MacRane*, you have a girl—a sweetheart?"

"No." Ralph didn't feel much like talking.

"War. Coming to an end. If you had a girl. You could see her soon I think. Your mother too."

Oh, to see his mother. The commandant had never before spoken like this.

A few days later, American B-29s were spotted over Japan. They looked like hulking green angels. They posed a serious threat to the soldiers and prisoners alike. Night after night, the men huddled in a shallow bomb shelter. It felt more like a mass grave. If a bomb were to strike close, it surely would be.

Despite the risks, the men were almost gleeful. They knew now that they were not alone, that they had not been abandoned. To see something built in America, to know it was coming for them meant the world. They cheered as bombs exploded nearby.

After a week of aerial bombing, the Americans started to mine the harbour. One twelve-hundred-pound mine missed the water, landing right beside the camp's guardhouse. The men were fearful they'd be forced to disarm it, but the commandant's behaviour was warming as the Americans closed in on him. He installed a soaker bathtub while a Japanese bomb squad removed the mine.

The war's cruelty was not quite over for the huddled men, though. Major Pulas—a captured American Marine—was caught waving to the U.S. planes as they passed overhead. Two guards scooped him out of bed and beat him mercilessly right outside the cabin door. He begged for them to stop. The dull end of two swords slammed into his back, his arms, his legs, and his hands. That was the last beating Ralph would recall.

The first morning that Major Pulas could get out of bed was the same morning that the foundry stacks were not smoking. This struck the men as impossible. Every morning the sun rose and the stacks smoked. It would take the foundry days to relight those fires in the belly of the plant. The men stood in the parade square being counted off, each looking at the stacks, then looking again. There really was no smoke. They'd be spared their daily hell for at least a few days. At the end of the count-off, the commandant confirmed what the men suspected: "No work today."

With Major Pulas's beating on their minds, the men tried hard not to smile. This would be a holiday unlike any they'd had.

Another day passed: no work. Then another. And another.

Then four days into their reprieve as slave labourers, they saw what they had prayed long and hard for: an American fighter bomber. They had seen the B-29s. A few of those had almost killed them. But this plane meant something entirely different, raising their spirits and their hopes.

The fighter planes were used by the U.S. Marines, and they flew from a nearby island base or an aircraft carrier. These were not long-range bombers. They didn't venture far. Their presence meant troops—American troops, lots of them.

The plane banked hard over the camp and hailed bullets across the fence, strafing everything in sight. The men's hearts beat hard in their chests as every foundry explosion brought them closer to their loved ones.

That was when Ralph finally allowed himself to believe. Staring at the foundry engulfed in flames, he thought to himself: *I am going to survive this.* The fire cleansed his heart. It scorched his anger. It lit a mighty hope in him. He was going to live. For the first time in five years, he was sure of it.

Most of the Japanese guards disappeared soon after the Corsairs were spotted. Only a few stuck around. Air raids become the norm. A few days later, Ralph awoke to screams of warning.

"Cover!"

"Incoming!"

Ralph scrambled out of his hut to dash to the bomb shelter. He saw two huge B-29s flying low as he ran across the parade grounds. There were no bombs going off in the harbour and the foundry had been destroyed. These B-29s were bearing straight for the camp.

"They *know* this is a POW camp. They know we are here. Right?" asked a man beside him in the shelter.

The men had painted a white cross on the mess hall. Was that enough? Would the pilots believe it? Everyone crouched and waited. Most prayed.

The plane's powerful engines screamed as it flew directly above the camp. Seconds of silence turned into one minute. A second minute passed. No explosions. At the three-minute mark, a few brave souls peeked out of the bomb shelter. Their view was glorious, but there were no cries of joy. The men were trying not to break down in tears. Dozens of forty-five-gallon barrels on parachutes were falling from the sky, blocking the sun. It was a supply drop. Leaflets hit the ground first. They were in Japanese, warning the guards of stiff penalties for withholding the supplies. The warnings were largely unnecessary as the men had free rein of the camp already. They piled out to chase the barrels as they fell. It was like keeping one's eyes on a snowflake.

Ralph remembered what a forty-five-pound barrel was capable of doing. He thought of his brother on the back of ol' Jack. He knew these barrels would save their lives once they came back to earth, but right now they were heavy objects hurtling through the air. They were deadly.

"Let 'em land! They're coming in fast!"

It was no use. You can't tell a starving man to wait in line.

Ralph stood watching helplessly as two men left through the gates, following one barrel. Like everyone, they had been ravaged by war, starvation, disease, and beatings. They were skeletons. They were blinded by these offerings. They stood in the field, arms outstretched, but the barrel was coming in too fast. It clipped one man and the weight of it crushed his skull. He was dead before the parachute softly furrowed onto the ground. His blood was smeared across the U.S. Army logo.

There was no time to grieve. The men had to nourish themselves. They opened the barrels and ate beef, cheese, crackers, chocolate. They ate whatever they could. All the while, they wept. The camp doctor warned the men that they would get sick if they ate too much. Their bodies were not prepared for the food. Having discharged his medical duty, he then proceeded to gorge himself.

Ralph found something even more important than food in his barrel. Placed between a row of canned peaches and army-issue blankets was a Gideon New Testament bible. It was as if it had been packed just for him. He ate the peaches but he clutched the bible. He was going to live and he was going to live by those words.

～～～

The war was over for the Japanese Imperial Army. The rumoured bomb was real, and while the men did not see the mushroom cloud, its effects were dramatic and immediate.

For the first time in years, every morning brought hope. It also brought a large breakfast. The men cooked powdered eggs, they fried canned meat, they drank coffee. They dipped eggs into ketchup. They remembered their mothers' kitchens and their local diners. For the first time, they thought with anticipation of friends and family. They would see their people again. They would hold loved ones in their arms. Each familiar taste, each nourishing bite brought them closer to that reunion. Not a dinner went by without someone openly sobbing. It was almost too much to handle all at once. The men were dining out on hope and lost love.

Several days later, after a large second helping of breakfast, and a bath, Ralph saw a group of men crowded around the main gate. As he approached, he saw two marines. They wore clean, dark green uniforms and polished black boots. They were shaven and each had a sidearm. Ralph held back tears as he heard one of them say, "Hang tough—we will have you out of here pretty quick. General McArthur is in Yokohama and the war is over."

Ralph had never, ever heard anything sweeter.

The crowd stayed, pressing the two airmen for more details. They had four years to catch up on. But Ralph had heard all he needed to hear. His war—his apocalypse—was over. He had seen the four horsemen and lived. He turned and walked straight to his hut. He got on his knees beside his bunk, clutched his bible, and thanked God for sparing him. He opened the bible and ran his fingers across a single passage, Mark 11:25: "And when you stand praying, if you hold anything against anyone, forgive him, so that your Father in heaven may forgive you your sins."

That afternoon, Major Pulas demanded that he be taken to Yokohama to meet with General McArthur.

It was another week before the men left the camp. There were no goodbyes. They marched out as they had marched in. This time, each had a smile on his face and a swelled heart in his chest.

At the train station, they began boarding for Yokohama. Ralph was near the back of the line. He heard a commotion, a voice. He knew who it was before he heard the words.

"MacRane! MacRane!"

How the tables had turned. Now Kato was just Kato. No commandant. No bowing. He weaved in and out among men whom a few weeks ago he would have beaten for not moving out of his way. He reeked of whisky. Having spotted Ralph in line, he rushed over. His bloodshot eyes were full of tears. He was wailing like a bull moose. He was defeated. He was scared.

Ralph genuinely believed that, more than anything, the commandant was sorry.

"MacRane." His shaky hands held out his pipe. He looked at Ralph, clearly hoping he would accept the gift.

"Here, here," Kato said, as he pressed his tobacco pouch into Ralph's hand. Then, Kato did something remarkable. He would have been killed for it if a Japanese officer had seen him. He ripped his rank stripes from the collar of his tunic. He placed them in Ralph's hand, on top of the pipe and tobacco pouch, and bowed deeply.

Ralph didn't know whether to throw a punch or offer an outstretched hand. He did neither. He closed his fist around the gifts, and looked Kato long and hard in the eye. He said nothing. He remembered the words of Mark 11:25, nodded, and boarded the train.

Thus ended four years and seven months of living under extreme duress—if you could call it living. Ralph had walked, slept, and eaten among the dead and dying. He had lost over half his body mass. He had been paralyzed twice, and blinded. His best friend had slipped through his fingers. He had been beaten and degraded. He had brushed up against his sanity on more than one occasion and stared down into the pit of death more times than he would care to talk about.

So, where could he go from there? How on earth could he move on?

The truth was, he already had.

CHAPTER 10

Amen

Ralph MacLean got off the boat in Vancouver on the same dock from which he'd left. An islander buddy by the name of Sid Street met him. They had a night. Such a night! He boarded the Canadian Pacific Railway train two days later, still a little hungover.

He took the same route Mitsue and Hideo had taken, across the Rockies, into the prairies. The train stopped in Calgary amid a throng of well-wishers. Among them was a young woman named Phyllis Dee. She was as shy as she was pretty. They didn't speak long, but it was all Ralph needed. As the train pulled out of the station, he stared at the address she had written down on his notepad. He thought about her all the way across the Canadian Shield. He was thinking about her still when he returned to the Magdalen Islands.

While his family smothered him with affection and he basked in it, he knew he could not stay. There was nothing there for him. The war had not changed that reality. He returned to Quebec City and was discharged on February 8, 1946. He wrote his mother and promised to send for her once he got himself set up out west. He was moving to Calgary.

Ralph started work at the Cominco smelter plant. Phyllis's father got him into the outfit. Ralph moved into Phyllis's family home until they could marry and build their own house. It took two years. They married on May 14, 1948, and moved into their house on Victoria Crescent. Then Ralph brought his mother to live with them in Calgary.

His younger brother, Ford, would visit, moving in and out of his home and his life. Ford was wild and always needed help. Ralph always obliged, until an incident happened that changed things.

Ralph had not heard from Ford in months, when one day the phone rang. He knew something was wrong the moment he picked up the receiver. He could hear Ford gasping on the other end.

"Ralphie—I'm in real trouble here," he said

Ford was in Regina, but he was on the run. He had been charged with rape. Ralph didn't ask if it was true. He didn't want to hear the words. He told his brother that he was sorry; this time, he just couldn't help him. It broke his heart to hang up.

Ford called once more, a week later. He told his older big brother that the girl he was accused of raping had been hit by a car and had died. The charges against him had been dropped.

The brothers didn't speak again for fifty years.

Ralph broke down sometimes. All the men who had been in the war did.

It was worst in the middle of the night, with his wife and three children asleep. He'd dream of electric feet, of poor Mortimer tied in the snow like an animal, of gunshots. He'd dream of Deighton. He'd see his friend's hands reaching towards him in the night. Come morning, Ralph would have trouble making his way to work. The downtown towers would turn to soot. They'd look like the foundry. He was driving into the war. He'd turn the car around and go back to bed. He would cry into his pillow.

Ralph's night terrors got much worse before they got better. It took him time to recover. It took medication. His bible helped. But Ralph did most of the heavy lifting himself. He never let himself get too far away from the prayer he had offered in the camp. He kept forgiveness close. It was his amen.

He worked at Cominco for forty years and twelve days.

Mitsue and her family were in Medicine Hat, still dealing with dust, heat, cold, and, at times, humiliation, but they were together. Hideo and her three children were her everything. They were her amen.

Until she too broke down, five years after the war's end. The dust, the isolation, the poverty had worn her down. In a desperate fit, she dressed Glory in a warm winter jacket and boarded a train back to British Columbia. She cried harder returning to Vancouver than she had leaving.

Being separated from her sons made her desperately unhappy, but she could not stay another night at the Golden Valley farm. She felt she had never left Coaldale, she still felt at war. She pleaded with Hideo to leave the farm. He promised he would. It took him two weeks to find and rent a house in Medicine Hat. The house, on 2nd Street, was tiny and old, but it was enough to get Mitsue to return. She never left again.

Part 4

The Gift

CHAPTER 11

The Gas City

My hometown is Medicine Hat, Alberta. We hear it all the time: it's a funny name. When government officials were first sent to the southeast corner of the Canadian prairies to determine its suitability for human life, they deemed it uninhabitable. It was altogether too hot, too barren, and too dusty to provide the basic needs of life.

The people of Medicine Hat did not want to be a sideshow, a prairie joke. They needed branding advice. They sought out the best. They wrote to their distant friend—Sir Rudyard Kipling, the Empire's poet. He was a man of the world. He understood the power of the word. He knew the industrious, the prosperous, people of import. From his vantage point in Sussex, surely Sir Kipling could tell them which alternate name was preferable: Leopoldville or Smithville. His expedited handwritten response shocked the council:

> To my mind, the name of Medicine Hat echoes the old Cree and Blackfoot tradition of red mystery and romance that once filled the prairies. Also it hints at the magic that underlies the city in the shape of your natural gas. Believe me, the very name is an asset, and as years go on will become more and more of an asset. It has no duplicate in the world; it makes men ask questions . . . and draws the feet of the young towards it; it has the qualities of uniqueness,

individuality, assertion and power. Above all, it is the lawful, original, sweat-and-dust-won name of the city and to change it would be to risk the luck of the city, to disgust and dishearten old-timers, not in the city alone, but the world over, and to advertise abroad the city's lack of faith in itself.

This remote outpost of the Dominion, wrote Sir Rudyard Kipling in 1908, "seems to have all hell for a basement, and the only trap door appears to be in Medicine Hat." He was referring, of course, to the large reserves of natural gas that gave the city its nickname, Gas City. He was gone as quickly as he arrived, but was not forgotten.

Medicine Hat it was. Medicine Hat it shall remain. It was the right call.

In 1912, evidence of Medicine Hat's growing economic prowess was erected to great fanfare. The town christened a large and imposing hotel, a four-storey, forty-six bedroom red-brick masterpiece across the street from the train station. Visitors were welcomed by a grand foyer, not unlike the one they would have just checked out of in the great hotels of Winnipeg. Every inch of the establishment was designed to exceed the expectations of the particular traveller. No expense was spared: lush carpets were laid on each floor, handsome brass bedsteads and chiffoniers were installed in each room. Guests could find a warm and welcoming dinner in the main floor dining room, which quickly won a culinary reputation second-to-none in western Canada. The men could retire with a cigar and a glass of imported scotch in the smoking room off the dining room. The proprietor, Mr. D. Broadfoot, a well-known hotel man, named his masterpiece Hotel Cecil. It was the town's crown jewel.

Hotel Cecil was a monument to Kipling's confidence in Medicine Hat. And it would feature largely in my future.

Forty-two years later, just down the road from the Cecil, on a crisp fall morning, Medicine Hat's first baby of Japanese descent was born. It was my father, Stanley Gene Sakamoto.

Medicine Hat was a kind town to my father. He did not have to fight his way through his childhood like his older brother Ron. If Ron inherited Mitsue's steely grit, my dad inherited her empathy. It seems a well deep enough to quench any need.

My dad is not of this time. Walking around Medicine Hat with him is like stepping into an episode of *King of Kensington*. It takes him an hour to go to the bank to make a simple deposit. He actually goes to the bank to speak to a teller. He does not have an Interac card. He has never used an ATM. Instead, he carries around enough cash in his fanny pack to buy a used car. Finally, as a caring family, we managed to convince Dad to limit his "walking around" money to a few hundred bucks, but the fanny pack is a bright red beacon. From his cold, dead hip shall we remove that fanny pack. We have tried our best to find him chic designs, but a fanny pack is still a fanny pack. He giggles as he clips it on in the foyer every afternoon.

In a strange way, he is also ahead of his time. Night after night throughout the early '90s, Dad would fall asleep with technology magazines forming a tent across his face. He knew about BlackBerrys and voice-recognition back when the technologies were still some-time off in the future, but he stubbornly refuses to relinquish his Motorola dumb phone for a smartphone. Instead, he carries around an actual phone book.

He usually puts three or four boxes of files into his Honda CRV for the day instead of using a laptop or an iPad. He does have a computer, but he uses it primarily for accessing Google Maps, where he can soar far above the clouds and wonder at it all. He has been able to bend and shape his world to suit his quirky ways. He goes to bed at 4 a.m. He wakes at noon. He is nocturnally nomadic, sleeping in various spots throughout the house, rarely returning to the same bed as the previous night. He giggles. A lot. A remnant of his time spent in the South Pacific, no doubt, his preferred wave is a *Hawaii Five-o*–style "hang loose." In Medicine Hat.

He is terrible, absolutely terrible, with names. His go-to names when he's in a jam are "big guy" or "shooter," whether it's a man or a woman. I have never seen him kiss anyone on both cheeks—that is too chichi. He does shake hands, but he prefers to thump the chest of the person he is greeting, just below the neck, with an open hand. Two or three thumps usually does the trick. Again, man or woman. It is the weirdest way I have ever seen a human being greet another. It is like he is in the wilds.

Dad plays in two hockey leagues: one where he is fifteen years older than everyone, one where he is the young buck at sixty-two. In both leagues, they call him Stan "Hackamoto" because he is the dirtiest player on the ice. He loves it. He taunts his opponents and hacks at the back of their legs if they get past him. He calls them unrepeatable names as they scramble for the puck in the corner. He giggles all the way down the handshake line after each game.

He has let his hair grow out and there is a lot of silver in it now. His face is getting rounder. He is looking more like his mom. I love calling him out of the blue, hoping to catch him when he is out and about. That's the best time. If he's on the road, he's all honks and waves. I know he has the phone cradled into his shoulder so as to not impede his ability to dish the "hang loose." If he's in a meeting, he always recounts the purpose in real time, as if I'm taking minutes. He ends those calls by telling me something interesting about the person he is meeting with: an upcoming event, a milestone reached, a granddaughter born. And that's it. That's why it takes my dad an hour to make a routine five-minute bank deposit. That's why people love to receive a "big guy," a "hang loose," a thump on the chest or a slash to the shins. That's why it doesn't matter if he doesn't know the names of most of the people he connects with on any given day. Because he actually connects.

When my dad speaks to you—in a bank lineup, a car wash, a restaurant—he is genuine in his desire to know about you. He doesn't give a shit about the weather. He knows it will change. He doesn't care to grumble about the latest political scandal. He knows that won't change. He wants to know about you. What is on your horizon, what you are proud of, excited for, fearful of. He collects intent and roots down to find the nugget of positive. He comes out of each mine with something. He is instinctively positive. He floats.

My parents met at a dance at McCoy High School in the fall of 1967. McCoy was—and still is—the town's one Catholic school. Even in my day, out of the dances of the three high schools, the McCoy dance was the one not to be missed. There was always a lot of repenting to be done the following Sunday.

Diane, my mom, had been cajoled to come down from Calgary for the dance by her cousin Darlene. She wore a green dress. They danced the night away to Sgt. Pepper's Lonely Hearts Club Band. Her parents didn't like rock 'n' roll, but they took in the comfort fact that the records coming through the front door were from their homeland.

My mom was cute. She had a light to her. Not a soft light—a hard light, like when a match is struck. Stan and Diane's romance flared. He was soon riding his 250cc motorbike north on Highway 1 to visit her in Calgary.

Darlene watched closely as Stan moved into her cousin's life. Everyone wondered how her father, Ralph, would react. The young man who was frequently sitting at his dining table, praying with him and passing him mashed potatoes, looked exactly like his tormentors of over twenty years ago.

Ralph watched Stan closely. He made sure he was polite. He made sure he treated his daughter—the apple of his eye—with respect and dignity. But remarkably, he never raised the issue of my father's race. Not once. He deemed my father very suitable. He even thought Diane lucky for finding such an honourable and upstanding young man. He approved mightily.

One day in the spring of 1968, Mitsue set the table. A special guest was coming. She brought out the good dishes. She guessed that the guest would begrudgingly have learned how to use chopsticks. But would he want to? For days she thought about what to serve. It kept her up at night. She had served many *hakujins* before, friends from the factory, neighbours, the kids' school friends. But never someone who had been imprisoned by the Japanese army. She decided on chow mein, sweet and sour spare ribs, barbecued B.C. sockeye salmon, and white rice.

She was scooping rice out of the Sanyo cooker when Ralph and Phyllis rang the doorbell. Hideo welcomed them in. Mitsue hurried into the living room, wiping her hands with a tea towel. They all shook hands and sat in the living room. *Senbei* crackers and almond chocolates were placed in a bowl on the oval living room table.

Mitsue and Ralph became instant friends. There was an unspoken understanding between them. They were both far too polite to state it, to address it. But they felt they knew each other. Deep down, they knew each other. They had both discarded the past, keeping only what they needed, leaving the rest behind. They did not compare hardships or measure injustices. They knew there was no merit to that.

They sat down at the dinner table. Hideo gave a toast. Ralph offered a prayer. They laughed. They could do that now.

Breaking down is the easy part. Anyone, at any time, can break down. The act of coming together again is what makes a hero. Moving on, with an open heart, seems, at times, impossible. But it's not.

~~~~~

I would not be born for another ten years, but that was the most important dinner of my life. Every story has two sides. My life depended on my sides coming together.

Thirty-three years later, the forgiveness that was shared that night would give me my life.

Dad graduated from the Southern Alberta Institute of Technology. He and my mom were married on December 29, 1973. His first job was as food and beverage manager at the Calgary Inn, and that is where the wedding, which included 150 guests, was held. Shortly after, Tom Brook, who was on the board of directors at the Inn and knew my dad, hired him as executive director at his new resort on Castaway Island in Fiji.

When they returned to Medicine Hat a year later, they bought a small duplex on Division Avenue, a busy street that divides the town into east and west. Our back yard was to the side of the house, encased in a three-foot wooden fence painted white and green. For the next few years, my father worked on the family farm and helped my uncle Ron with his music business. But what he always wanted was to have his own restaurant. In the fall of 1980, along with a few business partners, he opened Maxwell's. The restaurant featured a decidedly upscale menu. It was the first place in town where you could buy lobster. The waiters would trot out the Caesar salad carts and make the dish for you right at the table. The tablecloths were white linen and each had a real flower in the centre. Enya was piped in over the stereo system. They had a La Cimbali espresso machine imported from Italy. When I ate there I felt that I was in a far-off metropolitan place like New York City or Los Angeles.

There was a cocktail lounge just off the lobby of the restaurant. It was aptly named Smokers and had stained glass windows with Picasso-like women smoking long cigarettes. They were the first stained-glass windows I'd ever seen outside a church. It always seemed to me kind of sacrilegious. When the lounge was closed, I'd scamper up onto a stool behind the bar to pour myself a Sprite out of the bar nozzle, adding the thick red grenadine nectar for an extra dose of sweetness.

Running a restaurant is an incredibly tough gig. It forces you to be different people: a host charming the guests, but also, at times, a gruff taskmaster with the staff. One part quality control, one part bouncer. Throw in the books, the wholesale orders, the power-drunk safety inspectors, and the guy at the end of the bar who swears he'll pay you next week—and it takes its toll. Also on my dad's mind all the time, although he never spoke of it, was the high interest rates on commercial loans. Not to mention the hours: my dad would leave the house at 9 a.m. to make sure lunch preparations were well underway and would not return until after last-call. The late nights were hard.

I would struggle to fend off sleep so that I could see my weary father as he wound down at the end of a long day. I'd hear him come in the front door and into the living room, switch on the television, and rustle about in the kitchen as he made popcorn. As soon as I heard "Heeeeere's Johnny!" I'd creep out of bed. I would tuck myself under my dad's arm and be asleep before the montage was over.

I was a peculiar kid. I would wear goggles around the house for no apparent reason. We had a little green turtle pool that would provide relief from the hot summer afternoon. While I never dunked my head in the water, I wouldn't go near it without my trusty goggles. Mom would even have to bring my goggles with us when we went to our favourite park—Central Park—just down the road from the duplex. That there was no pool, just an old swing set and a concrete slide in the shape of whale, seemed unimportant to me.

My brother Daniel came along in the fall of 1980. He was a rugged-looking baby. "He's my Eskimo-baby," Mom would say proudly, if inappropriately. Daniel was born without fear of personal danger or potential harm.

Mom called Daniel and me her "bookends." The handle was well-earned. Most nights, while dad was still at work, we awoke and made our way down the hall, past the spare bedroom and the bathroom, to Mom. We'd scamper up into the bed and snuggle in tight. She'd shift a little, wrap an arm around each of us, and drift back to sleep. Sometimes Daniel and I would make the trek together, sometimes on our own. But every morning, there we were, on either side of her. Bookends.

Dad was usually too bone-tired to lug both of us back to our respective beds at the other end of the hall. Instead he'd sleep in my single bed, feet hanging over the end. We'd wake up with Mom and she would give us each a big squeeze. Even at one hundred and fifteen pounds, she managed to give one hell of a squeeze. As with everything else she did, she threw herself into those moments. She'd draw us both close and embrace us, then push us out in front of her by our shoulders to look us square in the eye and say three dear words: *I love you*. What a way to start the day.

After breakfast Daniel and I would walk through the tree-lined park, past the Mac's convenience store and up the hill to Webster Niblock Elementary School, knowing exactly where we stood with our mom. Our town knew where it stood with our mom too. If there was something she didn't quite like, she changed it. Like when she started the city S.P.C.A. to provide shelter for the animals she loved so much. Or when she established a private kindergarten when she deemed the city-run one not up to snuff.

Morningtime was Dad-time. Living with him was like living with Buddha. I've seen him visibly upset only a handful of times. I'm sure he has, but I cannot recall him ever once raising his voice to me. He usually walked around with a knowing smile. He was calm, like a monk's reflection pond. If you watched him closely, you'd see him inhale deeply, exhale deeply with each breath. He was in a state of perpetual meditation. He thought of time in decades.

On mornings in the summer, Daniel and I would wait until after we had eaten our peanut butter toast and finished watching *Mr. Rogers* and then we'd pounce. We'd usually tiptoe down the hall and sneak into our bedroom—where Dad had crashed at 2 a.m. the night before.

Light would be emerging through our baby blue A-Team drapes. We'd creep onto Daniel's bed and from this vantage point leap on Dad in unison. We'd hit him right in the midsection. We were little boys, but our combined weight would have pained the unprepared and he'd wake with an "Ohhh." He must have been playing along. He would have heard our clumsy little feet on the floor, the turn of the knob, our excited whispers. He'd wrestle us, smash us together in a brother pretzel, wrapping my arm over Daniel's head, his leg around my waist. He'd do so using the same theatrics we would see in the bootlegged Japanese sumo tapes we'd watch with Grandpa Sakamoto. It was all bug eyes, fast hands, and wails of "yooooough." We'd pretend we couldn't breathe, just so he'd let go and reconfigure our limbs all over again. He'd usually had about five hours of sleep.

Dad would rise in his underwear and undershirt and flick on the Mr. Coffee Automatic in the kitchen. I remember him moving slowly, much more slowly than Mom in the morning. He was never a morning guy.

He'd throw on jeans and a T-shirt. He was partial to the three-quarter-length-sleeved variety. His favourite at the time had black sleeves and the Rolling Stones bright red lips and tongue splashed across his chest. Mom hated it. She thought it was vulgar and she hated the colour red. She was funny that way. She hated the crinkling sound of potato chip bags, smacking lips while chewing gum, and the colour red. But with her at work and his suit neatly pressed in his office at the restaurant, Dad was free to wear what he liked. Mick Jagger it was.

The three of us would pile into his beige 1974 Chevy half-ton, equipped with an oversized white camper appointed with fake wood panelling and four windows. The camper was fastened to the truck's cab by cables that hooked under the wheel wells. The thing never seemed to fit and we never once used it to camp. I suppose my dad kept it to use on the farm. The problem was, anytime we needed shelter from the scorching prairie sun, that aluminum box was a torturous sweatshop. In every picture I have ever seen of us on the farm we are outside—unsheltered—taking a break by the truck.

Despite all that, Daniel and I loved driving in that truck, where we could be fairly mistaken for wolf pups. As soon as we hopped into the cab, we would open our mouths as wide as we could and bite into the padded dashboard. Our teeth imprints lined the dash from the eight-track player clear to the passenger side window. The cab of Dad's truck looked like an orthodontist's mould, though an orthodontist would have been appalled at the risk we were running. We were one quick brake away from losing every tooth in our heads.

As we perched there with eyes peering just over the dashboard and drool coming out of our gaping mouths, Dad would shake his head, fire up the engine, and back out of the driveway. The drop from the sidewalk to the road would sink our teeth a little deeper into the dash padding. The next twenty-five seconds were the most important of the day—everything else hinged on them. We watched for any sign of what was to come next. Was Dad looking right or left? He never signalled as he approached the end of our street, a T intersection. A left turn led to Grandma Sakamoto's, a right led to the babysitter's. We would chant "left" which actually came out against the dashboard as "eff."

We went to bed hoping for a left turn. We woke up hoping for a left turn. A left meant Grandma's. As we went through the motions of morning, we were envisioning the truck turning left, following the park to 12th Street, and winding down the hill into Riverside. We usually did turn left, which meant ice cream sandwiches, *inari* sushi, ginger ale, puzzles, plastic army men, *senbei*, Stampede wrestling on TV, hamburgers with home-cut fries, and ninja movies.

By 4:15, Mom would be there to pick us up. If our shoes were muddy, she knew we had been down by the river. If we had the spears of prairie grass embedded in our corduroy pants, it was the tracks. She'd have none of our biting antics of the morning. We didn't dare. Despite her slight build, she kept us in line with military precision. When she took us to her hair salon, she'd instruct the stylist to give us the RCMP cut. She did not suffer bad behaviour gladly; she didn't suffer it at all. She rooted it out and exterminated it with extreme prejudice. What she believed in, more than anything, was love, but it was a tough love.

At 5 p.m. when we walked into the house and into the kitchen, we always wished we were still at Grandma's. Mom was a lot of things, but a great cook was not one of them. Lunches consisted of microwaved brown beans or boiled Ichiban. Snack time, morning or night, was always peanut butter on toast. By day's end, dinner was usually a hill too high for Mom to climb. We often ended up at a restaurant. Sometimes it was Dad's, sometimes it was the local pizza joint, Farroh's, where pizza came with a round dough bun in the middle that Daniel and I would call dibs on. The Oriental was our other likely destination. Every prairie town has a Chinese restaurant just like it. Heaping plates of beef and broccoli, and chicken fried rice with frozen vegetables.

The three of us would carefully count each shrimp on the oyster-sauce-laden platter. Mom made sure her two boys got their equal share of shrimp. An equal share of her attention. An equal share of her. Her bookends could have been scales. She did not play favourites. That's not to say she treated us the same. She tailored her parenting for each of us. With me, she knew she just had to let it be known that she was disappointed in my behaviour. She would lightly slap the top of my hand if I touched a bottle of bleach or handled a steak knife. I would not do it again. Daniel she could have beaten black and blue to no avail. There was just no fear in that boy. He was always on the move. So she would take away his mobility. Daniel had a time-out seat in the corner of our room. It killed him to sit still for fifteen minutes. He'd do anything to avoid it. Mom knew her boys; she knew how to motivate, strike fear, cajole, and inspire.

Once a month, we'd make our way up the Number One Highway to Grandpa MacLean's house. Grandpa had built his home with his own hands. It was a large house, in impeccable shape. He had a flagpole in the front yard and the Canadian flag flew high. As soon as we went in the side door, we would run downstairs to the games room. It had 1950s tiling on the floor and Mom's old novels on the shelves. At the far end of the room was an ornamental oak mantel that displayed black and white pictures of row after row of headstones. There was a commemorative plaque in English and Chinese. There were three medals affixed to a wooden board. Hung at the top of the wall was a map of my grandpa's distant island home.

Grandpa, Daniel, and I would spend all day playing chess. Daniel and I made a good team; he being brave, me being cautious. But we knew Grandpa was letting us win.

I could have used some of Daniel's bravery when the time came for me to head off to Grade 1. I was the one yellow kid in a sea of

white kids. My mom walked me to school that first day. I wore blue jeans, a blue buttoned-up shirt, and a blue backpack. But I was yellow, a pale yellow. However, I was blissfully unaware of this. I loved Hubba Bubba, Star Wars, and 7-Eleven slushies like any other kid. I knew my brother and I were half Japanese and that made us a little different. But before school, I was always around kids like me. My brother, my cousins, the Hashizume kids, the Nishimotos, the Hashiguchis. I saw similarity on a daily basis. At Webster Niblock, I was all alone. There were twenty-four kids under that roof. I was the only kid who wasn't white.

As we stood up for roll call, "Sakamoto" caused a few snickers. I looked different, but not that different. I was, after all, half Japanese, half Scottish. Most kids could not quite put their finger on it.

Daniel and I were the youngest kids on our block and, not surprisingly, street hockey was the sport of choice. All the big kids would stake out their hero: "I'm Wayne!" "I'm Lanny!" I'd always be the last to yell: "I'm Matt!" Matt Kabayama never made it to the NHL, but he was one of the finest WHL players Medicine Hat ever produced. He was a slight Japanese kid living in a world of burly white farm kids. I related.

The year I was in grade 1, my dad put me in hockey. At the beginning of the season, we went to Black's Sports down on 2nd Street to get me suited up with size-six Braun skates, a helmet, and a wooden Koho stick that he cut down to size in the driveway as soon as we got home. He made sure that the helmet had a full mask. It was a white cage around my face. I was too excited to sit still long enough to bite the dashboard on the way home. Matt Kabayama, here I come!

At my first practice, Dad suited me up. He hunched over and did my laces up. It felt like he tied them too tightly, but I didn't say anything. I walked slowly down the padded aisle, holding the cinderblock wall to keep my balance. I was shaky hitting the ice. I tried to remember the drills Dad had run me through on the open Riverside rink. But my knees kept on folding in on themselves. I was up and I was down. I'd see ice and then I'd see the rink's roof. I was glad for the helmet.

At one point I was happy to be leaning my back against the boards by the penalty box. A boy skated in front of me and looked hard through my facemask. Even behind the white cage, I looked different from him. But like the kids at Webster Niblock, he couldn't quite place me. He stared for a long moment, blinking, taking me in. Then, eureka!

"You're a nigger."

I'd never heard the word.

"I don't think I am." This was a statement of fact.

Then the whistle blew and we were off to do our drill. I felt as visible as the bright orange pylons I was unsuccessfully trying to navigate. I held my tears back as we drove the seven blocks home from the Crescent Heights rink. Dad did not press me.

Back home, I threw my face into my pillow and cried. Mom let me cry for a few minutes to get it out. She wanted to be sure I would hear what she had to say.

"Get up."

I did.

"Look at me." There was no softness. There was no pity.

She was standing in the doorway. Her hands were on her hips. Her eyes were on fire.

"It doesn't matter what colour your skin is, so long as it's thick."

That was that. She closed the door to let me ponder that, cry some more, whatever. She knew I had got the message.

CHAPTER 12

Breakup

Mom did her best to instill in me a warm heart. Many mornings as I walked into the kitchen, she would beckon me over to her favourite spot at the table, the spot where the morning light shone through the window and warmed her morning tea. She'd tell me every morning that my heart was golden.

She believed in her boys. It was contagious. We felt we could, *we really could*, do whatever we wanted. Our reach was only limited by our imagination.

When Daniel turned three, Mom began working full time as a receptionist at City Hall. Her re-entry into the workforce called for a fashion makeover. She called in a heavy-hitter, her friend Donna Stetic; they had worked together at the Department of Community Services and Recreation.

Donna seemed distinguished to me. She had no children. She was like the ladies of means I'd see on mom's soap operas. She was in her early forties and she acted her age. Her husband owned a large cattle ranch forty miles east of the city. Mom came home from the fanciest store in town—Friday's Image—with a purple satin blouse with shoulder pads, purple pleated slacks, a green jumpsuit, three pairs of high heels, one pearl necklace and a flower brooch. She was so excited she had worn the jumpsuit home.

Strangely for a Canadian, I remember summers far more than winters. Every weekend, we would hop into our dad's brown Chevy truck and make our way to the farm. It was just a few minutes south of town. The farm was sixty-two acres of cukes, tomatoes, potatoes, and corn. The north side was lined with massive spruce trees, but to the south you could see until the end of time. Growing up under a wide-open sky profoundly affects your outlook. You feel boundless.

Daniel and I, too young to be enlisted into hard labour like our older cousins, spent most of our days playing in the cornfields. The tall husks were perfect for hiding and seeking, attacking and retreating. We made good use of our time, knowing full well that the very corn that was our disguise would soon become our chore. In a few months, we would be sitting on Grandma and Grandpa Sakamoto's driveway husking truckloads of corn that never seemed to end. We didn't dare complain. We knew how hard everyone else was working.

While my world was expanding, my parents' marriage was diminishing. They were speaking less. Their conversations became mechanical, bureaucratic. Who is taking what, where? My dad had never been chatty, preferring to let his actions speak for him. He wrote his thoughts down in a three-ring binder that he stashed on the top shelf of our foyer. I knew this because I'd see my mom drag a kitchen chair into the front lobby and pull the binder down to read his thoughts. I would sneak peeks myself. Most of his entries were about his failing business: he was losing Maxwell's.

That September, when I was seven years old, I bought Dad a pen for his birthday, hoping to make him feel better.

Two weeks later, Mom began crying almost hysterically.

"Just looook at this kitchen!" she screeched as she ran her hands through her frosted hair.

The portable dishwasher, full of dirty dishes, was hooked up to the kitchen tap. She hadn't found the time to turn it on. The sink was full of three days' worth of soaking pots and pans. Burnt crusts clung to the parts sticking out of the oil-tinged brown water. A few remaining soap bubbles hung in each rounded corner of the stainless steel sink. A mountain range of soccer jerseys, jeans, T-shirts, underwear, and socks sat beside the fridge waiting to be carried downstairs to the washing machine. Each day the pile grew. The fridge was near empty. Four utility bills and one mortgage statement were posted on the fridge—a constant reminder of our arrears.

Daniel and I sat at the kitchen table, watching, waiting for supper, unsure what to do. Dad was working—he was always working. Mom was alone. She paced the kitchen like a caged animal.

She went to the bathroom to get some toilet paper to blow her nose. Nose still runny, she marched back into the kitchen, grabbed an empty Kleenex box, and threw it to the ground. We were out of paper products.

"My mother NEVER ran out of toilet paper!" Mom burst into tears again and slumped onto the kitchen floor, her back against the dishwasher, defeated. Daniel ran to the stove, grabbed the small kitchen towel, and handed it to her. "Don't cry, Mom. It's okay."

It was not okay. Mom decided, at that very moment, I think, that life could not go on like this. It had to get better. We needed a cleaner house. We needed more food in the fridge. We needed toilet paper. I remember the look in her eyes. She was determined to go it alone.

The next night, I lashed out at my father. We were at grandma Sakamoto's for dinner. Mom was not there. I was sitting on the kitchen counter, between the telephone and the sink. I was mad because he was not home when Mom was in need. I was mad that we had an empty fridge, a messy house, and past-due bills. I was mad that we didn't have toilet paper. I lay in wait for an opening.

He asked me a simple, fatherly question. Something like "How was your day?"

"What do you care, you're never around," I said sulkily.

I may have as well have taken out one of Grandma's *santoku* knives and stabbed him.

"Don't you ever say that to me again," he replied, his firmness masking his pain.

I jumped off the counter and ran to the guest room, leaped onto the bed, and plunged my face into the pillow. Dad probably felt like doing the same.

I think I have relived this moment more than any other. If I could take back but one sentence in my life, corral the words, and choke them back into my mouth, that would be the one.

That week, during one of her 10:45 a.m. coffee breaks, Mom decided to end her marriage. She informed grandma Sakamoto that very afternoon at 4:15 p.m., when she arrived to pick us up. Grandma broke down and wept. She begged her to reconsider, but Mom would not be moved. It was decided. She loaded us into the car and we were off.

Mom and Dad sat my brother and me down in our living room to tell us. The sun shone through the blinds against the bay window. Mom did the talking, Dad sat ashen-faced. He looked like he just wanted to wake up from a bad dream.

Afterwards I fled to the park across the street, climbed a tree, and stared at my house. At eight, I was old enough to know life was about to alter dramatically. I felt fear for the first time.

As far as divorces go, theirs was quite amicable, although we must have been shielded from some of the ugly moments that are bound to occur as two people unwind their life together. I recall only one screaming match, an early morning fight in the bathroom that woke me up. As I came out of my bedroom, I saw my dad standing in the hall, staring into the bathroom. "You go to hell," he said with tears in his eyes. I had never heard my dad curse. I had never seen him cry.

Three weeks later, we were all packing up: Dad to move to a rented house not far from our first place on Division Avenue, Mom,

Daniel, and I to a duplex just around the corner and across the street from a subsidized housing complex. Mom had borrowed the down payment from grandpa MacLean. She hated to do so. She would rather owe the bank than her dad, but a single mother with a receptionist's salary didn't make for an ideal loan candidate.

The fear that had introduced itself to me in the tree became a constant companion. The ground under our feet had shifted. Like an earthquake survivor, I spent my days on edge, waiting for the next tremor.

Mom never really did articulate her reason for divorcing Dad. I think she needed release. She needed to feel truly free. But she was walking a tightrope without a safety net. Her first steps out onto the wire were unsteady.

On the surface, many things remained the same. Our morning routine was unchanged: waking up to a hug, breakfast cereal at the kitchen table, Mom watching us as she sipped Earl Grey tea. Off to school, home for lunch—Ichiban soup—babysitting Daniel from 3:10 until 4:45 p.m., when Mom returned. She watched *Oprah* in the living room from 5 to 6 p.m. while Daniel and I played with the neighbourhood kids. Then dinner, clean-up, homework at the kitchen table, *The National* newscast, and off to bed. Pretty routine stuff.

But cracks began to appear. I kept my eye on them like a home inspector, hoping they wouldn't impact the foundation. As I watched the small cracks grow, I wondered if anyone else saw them.

In the new place, although my bedroom was downstairs and Daniel's upstairs, we continued to sleep together. Old habits die hard. In bed at night, we would tap each other on the leg with our feet. One tap meant you weren't tired; five meant you were close to sleep. It should have been the other way around, but that's how we did it. We only started to do that after the divorce. We were scared; we had reason to be. In the half-light, we knew things were changing. We knew our mom was changing.

At first, the tiny duplex took on the feel of a chaperoned teenage party. A new cast of friends came into my mom's life. For the most part, they were a fun-loving, motley crew. Most were divorcees or folks in transitory stages of life.

A woman named Terry moved into the duplex next door. She was also a recent divorcee and she lived with her son, Wade. A pretty woman with a vibrant laugh, she had that late-80s sex appeal down pat. She drank fruit wine coolers and blared "Walk Like an Egyptian" in the afternoon.

Jerry was a neighbour who lived up the street. He liked to push the limits. He drove a fast car too fast. His favourite pastime was stabbing his hunting knife between his (or someone else's) outstretched fingers. He was a dead ringer for Sting. At least once a month, he'd receive a free lunch somewhere in town because the server thought he was the rock legend. Jerry would never dispel their misconception. He would tell the waitress he was on a meditation retreat.

There was a good-looking man who wore a very old and very cool jean jacket. He rode a motorcycle and had the confident ease of a guy who has been cool all his life. He didn't flaunt it, but you knew it, and he knew you knew it. But as a father with two young girls and a wife at home, he was finding life was quickly becoming less cool. With him, you knew something was going to give.

Rounding out the group was a fun-loving, carefree guy named Mike who rented a basement bedroom from Terry. Born on an aboriginal reserve in northern Alberta, Mike had spent his early adulthood trying to cram as much joy into his life as he could, trying to make up for lost time. In college, he started a Hug Society, where volunteers manned a booth and gave a hug to anyone who would take one. Like a man back from the desert with an insatiable thirst, Mike could not get enough affection.

They danced, they laughed, they drank. They were merry.

I was nine years old. The antics of my mom's new friends excited me. We would have water fights in the backyard. We would all hop into a caravan and head to Echo Dale park, a man-made beach. The women would sunbathe while the guys played Frisbee. On one occasion, Mike gingerly untied Terry's bikini top as she slept face down on her outstretched beach towel. He then called her to ask if she wanted to go swimming. She got up and bounced half-way to the water before realizing she was the star of a burlesque show. Her scream only drew more attention as she dashed back to the safety of her towel. I sat, mesmerized, as her large milk-white breasts bounded in front of me. I had never seen real live breasts before. After the commotion died down, the gang decided to go for ice cream at the concession. I opted to stay lying on my towel.

Every weekend seemed to herald another party. A month after Terry moved in, there was a well-worn path between the duplexes. Revellers moved back and forth between two sides of the same party. Sometimes other children were around, sometimes not. Without a bedtime, and given our mom's penchant to include us, we were just part of the festivities; in on (most) of the jokes, singing along, dancing in the living room, drinking iced tea instead of vodka coolers. I have pictures of my mom, laughing, wine glass in one hand, her arm around my shoulder, bunching my '86 Expo T-shirt up at the collar.

Invariably, they'd decide to find a place to go for last call. I hated it when they left for the bar. Deemed old enough to look after my five-year-old brother, I was still afraid of the dark. I would get Daniel into his Superman pyjamas and settled into bed. He'd usually fall asleep quickly. I'd just lie there, eyes wide open, scared of the creaks in the basement and the voices I could hear in the back alley. Scared that my mom was becoming less and less my mom by the day.

Sometimes, if it got too late, or I got too scared, I would quietly get out of bed. Mom would always leave the name of the bar and the phone number on the table in the kitchen. I knew each name: Cadillac's, the country bar on the other side of town; Moby Dick's, the English pub at the bottom of the hill; Mario's, the downtown bar in the basement of an Italian restaurant. If she hurried, Mom could be home from Cadillac's in fifteen minutes, Mario's in seven, and Moby Dick's in five.

I'd sit at the table and vacillate while I twirled the thick black spiral phone cord. Finally I'd dial.

A gruff voice would answer. The bartender must have struggled to hear me whisper, "Is Diane Sakamoto there?" over the sound of the patrons yelling, laughing, and ordering drinks and the twang of the slide guitar.

"Who? You gotta speak up."

I couldn't or Daniel would wake up and be scared that Mom was not home yet. I was his older brother, but still not old enough to exude the kind of reassurance that he needed.

I would cup my hand around the black receiver and repeat "Diane Sakamoto" in as loud a whisper as I could.

"Yeah, I just saw her. Hold on." Medicine Hat was a small town. Bartenders knew everyone in their establishment.

"Di—your kid's on the phone," I would hear him call over the bar.

Moments later I'd hear "Hi, Mark, everything okay?"

I remember always being relieved to hear her voice; to be connected with her again.

"Are you coming home soon?" I'd ask.

"Yes. I'm just finishing up here."

She was always just finishing up. She was never just finishing up. I knew it. There was always just one more glass of wine.

There would be a silence between us. There was really nothing else to say, and I was always mad at myself for having made that futile attempt. I was mad at my mom for not being with us, for lying to me, for leaving me. I knew, deep down, that my mom *was* leaving me. I think that was why I never wanted to hang up the phone. I would stand there in silence, phone to my ear, listening to her breathe on the other end of the line, the music and banter in the background. She would let the silence persist for a long time too. Maybe she felt the same way.

For a period of about six months, we would do this every weekend. She at the bar in her jumpsuit and high heels, me at home in my pyjamas. Lingering on the phone just before last call. Neither of us wanting to disconnect. Both knowing we would. Each goodbye a small one on a long road of goodbyes.

"Go to bed, sweetheart. I'll be home shortly."

"Please come home soon, okay?"

"I will, darling."

She'd hang up the phone and I'd sit at the kitchen table alone, knowing she'd ordered another drink. Cigarette ashes, beer, and vodka-cooler bottles would be strewn in front of me.

Of course with the weekly parties, things got complicated. One day, after a particularly late evening, Mom was making Daniel and me pancakes when a blue minivan stormed up our driveway. I scrambled to the window to see the van half on our driveway and half in the hedge that lined it. Mom knew who it was without looking out the kitchen window.

"Into my bedroom, boys. Now."

I could hear a woman's voice screaming from outside as the minivan door slammed shut. I recognized it immediately. "Diane, you bitch. Send my husband out here. You slut!"

It was nine in the morning, but this woman's world was coming undone and she had lost all care for manners somewhere in the wee hours of her sleepless night. She was thinking about her little girls, about her husband's betrayal. She wasn't thinking. She was acting on instinct. I heard the latch click as my mom opened the door just a fraction. The woman's voice echoed through our house. Horrid words spewed up the stairs from the landing as our pancakes got cold. My mom kept calm.

"There are two sides to this duplex, dear."

Mom's bedroom shared a wall with Terry's next door. Through the wall I could hear two people frantically moving about, getting dressed. Mom opened her bedroom door. Daniel and I must have been wide-eyed, because she immediately kneeled beside the bed and brought us both close.

"It's fine—let's go back to breakfast," she said.

From the living room window I saw the woman get back into

her minivan. She backed it out of our hedge. The cool guy with the jean jacket followed on his motorbike.

Then Mom met a new man.

CHAPTER 13

Breakdown

Stephen introduced me to violence.

I was a fireproof house. I had been untouched by it, never close to it. I never suspected it. I never saw it coming.

Life took a decidedly dark turn when Stephen came into Mom's life. Her party with Terry and the gang ended as abruptly as it had begun. Mom met Stephen at Moby Dick's Tavern. She was forty, he was twenty-eight. He lived with his mother just around the corner from the bar, above a dry cleaner.

Stephen was a well-built, clean-cut man with sinewy muscles. He had a moustache and wore dark glasses that shaded his eyes from view. He drove a gun-metal grey Chevy Beretta. It had racing stripes and it was fast. The first time we met, he took me out on the service roads to the north of town in the light industrial area. The roads there are well paved and, given the prairie landscape, you can see an approaching car miles away. We spent the afternoon pretending to be stock-car racers.

Their relationship moved as fast as his car. Mom was racing my dad in getting on with life. Stephen moved in shortly after they met. He and Mom were married even before all his CDs were unpacked.

Living with Stephen was like having a new roommate around. We got a better stereo system with new CDs, mostly stuff from the '70s: Cat Stevens, Jethro Tull, Led Zeppelin. The '70s were Stephen's glory days.

Soon after the wedding, on a sunny Saturday afternoon, Mom and I were in the kitchen having lunch. Daniel was out with Dad that afternoon. Stephen was listening to The Black Crowes in the living room and smoking hand-rolled cigarettes. He hadn't said much all day. Mom told me he was in a mood. I didn't quite know what that meant, but I understood I was to lie low, like you'd see in the movies when someone stumbled onto a bear or a cougar. It felt like we had a wild animal in the house. No quick movements. Avoid eye contact. No rash noises. Be slow and careful. That was the way to act. Hopefully, he'd just move on.

Nope.

Stephen got his campaign of violence underway. He declared war with a long, guttural growl. I don't recall what set him off, though it could have been absolutely anything. I remember the sound emanating from the living room. Then I heard him leap off the couch. He landed with a thump, so he must have flung himself into the air. He was around the corner before I was even standing. He was in a rage. He was shouting, baring his teeth.

Mom stood up to brace herself against his assault. Unsure what to do, I stood beside her. We hugged each other as he circled around us—pacing, stalking. There was vodka on his breath. I remember his spit hitting my face as he came in close. We said nothing. I felt my mom's heart pounding. I felt my heart pounding. My mouth was dry and I tasted metal. I had never been exposed to anything like this before. I hung onto my mom as if she were a tree in the middle of a storm.

Stephen punched the fridge twice and left the house. He peeled out of the alleyway. I could hear rocks hitting our fence.

Mom sat down and lit a cigarette. Her hands were shaking. I remained just where I was, shell-shocked. Then I walked into the living room and picked up a pillow that had fallen off the couch. I stood in the centre of the room. Somehow it looked different.

Stephen returned two hours later and went into the bedroom. There was not a sound for another two hours. Mom and I held our breath. Otherwise she tried to act as if nothing had happened. She made dinner.

Stephen came out of the bedroom. Mom was still in the kitchen, and I was alone in the living room, eating spaghetti and watching CNN. He was a different person. The storm had passed. He declared a truce; he apologized for his behaviour. He said he was sorry if he had scared me; he would never act like that again.

That night, at the age of twelve, I learned what terror was. I learned what it felt like to know your enemy.

And so, the predictable cycle of unpredictable violence began. Every few months the fighting would erupt. Stephen would harm my mom. He would shove her to the ground. He would lord over her. He would slap her. He wanted her to know who was boss. She was the only thing he could control and he set about doing it completely.

Invariably, the police would arrive at the scene. Mom would have called, or a neighbour. Stephen would spend the night in the city jail.

Their lifestyle was a one-way road. In a matter of months, Mom lost her job at City Hall. She had been coming in to work smelling of cigarettes and cheap wine. She would go days without bathing. Alcohol and abuse were her constant companions. She was losing herself, losing her dignity. Her world was closing in on her.

As my mom was sinking, my dad was finding some ground beneath his feet.

One night in the dead of winter, he told us to grab our skates. We hopped into his green Pontiac Parisienne and made our way to Strathcona Park and a man-made pond created from water diverted from the South Saskatchewan River just before it passed through town. The pond ice was bumpy, but the pavilion had better hot chocolate than any of the other city rinks. I ran ahead while my dad helped Daniel from the car. As I was lacing up in the skate shack, a pretty woman in a purple jacket approached me. She said hi and told me that she knew my mom and dad. I remember being a little rude; I was in a hurry to hit the ice. Her name was Susan.

Daniel and I sat side by side on the wooden plank bench. As always, Dad inspected our laces. He retied them tight. It felt like he had superhuman strength when he hunched over the way dads do at rink-side. Then we were off.

The ice by the pavilion had been shovelled and so had a path that circled the island in the middle of the pond. It was dark, but the street lamps poured a soft orange light across the falling snowflakes and the ice. There were only a few kids out that night. You could see the whole pond. Daniel and I became engrossed in a game of tag. I looked up to see Dad and the woman I had just met skating hand in hand around the island. The orange light made her purple jacket look red.

Susan had four boys, two from a marriage that had ended long ago. She was eighteen when she had Cameron. Her father had forced her to marry. Two years later, she had Chad. A few months after his birth, her husband ran off with her best friend. When he returned the next week, the locks had already been changed. A few years later she married Bob Dennison. A kind and bright man, Bob was an accountant. Bob loved numbers and he loved Paul Simon. They had a son, Carrick, and were happy. But just before Susan gave birth to their second son, Logan, a darkness befell her. She worried endlessly about the unborn baby. Logan was a healthy boy. But a tragedy was coming.

Bob died of cancer before Logan turned three.

Carrick was Daniel's age. He had a red cowlick and, at nine, shared his father's love for Paul Simon if not his love for numbers. He and Daniel soon became thick as thieves.

Susan had been a mother her entire adult life, and she welcomed two more boys into her home. She lived in a house she had designed herself on the very edge of town, the fanciest part. The first time we went there, each home along her street seemed a castle larger than the next. Her back deck spanned the entire house. From it, the view was of nothing. Just a deep prairie valley. No neighbours, save a few antelope and stalking coyotes. Train tracks hugged the valley basin.

We spent the summer wading through the creek, tracking animals, and hiding from farmers patrolling their plots. By summer's end, the single beds in the two basement bedrooms had been removed and bunks put in. By then, Susan had been dating my dad for thirty weeks. We were welcome there anytime. In her home, around her dinner table, and in her heart, there was always room for more. Soon after Dad and Susan added a baby girl to our newly formed band of brothers. They named her Kumiko Suzanne.

Dad went back into the food business. Porky Smith retired and the Medicine Hat Stampede Board called to see if Dad wanted to take over the business. He started a catering company called Shooting Star Events. He won business from the Stampede Board, three high schools, and most of the major oil companies. The first event he catered was McCoy High's graduation.

Dad found a way to recreate the immigrant experience in the back kitchen of the Cypress Centre hall. He put his boys to work scrubbing through three thousand plates, fifteen hundred forks, and three thousand saucers. At 1 a.m., when we thought we were done, Pete, a lovable guy with more than a couple of brushes with the law, unloaded fifteen one-hundred-pound cauldrons from his Chevy Camino. It was all Carrick, Daniel, and I could do to get them loaded into the sink for scrubbing. We didn't leave that night till 4 a.m. We were drenched. Every part of my body was wrinkled like a raisin. We had been on the receiving end of a thirteen-hour gravy-fuelled steam bath in that dish pit.

As we piled into Dad's Chevy Suburban, he chuckled. *Education, boys, education. Make sure to get one*, he said. Our professional lives could only go up from there. At home we climbed into our bunk beds and listened to Paul Simon's "Train in the Distance" as a train passed through the prairie valley.

So long as Mom was sober, Carrick was allowed to sleep over at our house. Our lives were converging. Daniel and I were becoming a unit of brothers in a myriad of units of brothers. Once again as our world expanded, Mom's closed in on her. Carrick's sleepovers became infrequent.

Daniel's upstairs bedroom was right next to Mom's. He heard all the fights, even the quiet ones. They were the worst. Growls would come from the bedroom. Sitting up in bed with his Edmonton Oilers pyjamas, Daniel would inch his back into the corner of the room. He would fall asleep fearfully gripping a hockey stick.

Finally he couldn't take it anymore. He knew he couldn't stay. He belonged at Dad's. He was safe at Dad's. He was eight, but old enough to take his life into his own hands. Mom had raised him well. He asked her to sit down at the kitchen table. She lit a cigarette and looked at him with anticipation.

"What is it?"

"I've decided to move in with Dad."

Tears welled in her eyes. She could muster only one more word. "Why?"

The day Daniel moved out, Mom was upstairs in her bedroom. I helped carry some boxes down to Dad's Suburban. Mom would not leave her room. She lay in a fetal position in the middle of the bed, her eyes wide open. Tears from her left eye rolled across the bridge of her nose. We didn't have Kleenex so she just kept a roll of toilet paper beside her. Every second box or so I carried, I'd pop in and rub her back. She didn't say a word.

When we were done, Daniel stood at the bottom of the stairs. He had tears in his eyes.

"Is she coming out?"

I didn't know.

Then we heard the bedroom door open. Mom had wiped her eyes and blown her nose, but the evidence was clear.

Ever the loyal mother, she put on her bravest face, tilted her head, and gave Daniel a warm and loving smile.

"I love you, my baby." She knelt down as Daniel ran up the stairs and hugged her.

Dad waited in the truck. His hands were on the steering wheel and his head was bowed. Four broken hearts were trying their best.

"I love you too, Mom," Daniel said.

When the front door closed, Mom collapsed at the top of the stairs. She wailed. I had never heard pain made audible like that. I hope I never do again.

She knew *why*.

After Daniel left, I took up a nomadic existence. I kept a bathroom kit and a pair of clean underwear in my school backpack. Some nights I'd stay with Mom. If the fighting got bad, I'd make my way to grandma Sakamoto's. Every third night or so, I'd stay at Dad's. It was no way to live. I knew that. My dad knew that. My mom knew that. I couldn't live with my mom, but I could not leave her. I was her oldest; I was supposed to help keep her safe. I was failing miserably. We both were.

I remained in that purgatory for years. Every day after school, I'd take the bus down to Riverside. Cale Turner and I would spend the afternoon eating taco chips in grandma Sakamoto's basement, talking about girls and Nirvana. After supper with Grandma, I'd call Mom. I would listen for clues: a slurred word; a yell in the background from Stephen. If she sounded sober, if it sounded safe, I'd walk up the Riverside bridge and stay at her house. If not, I'd call Dad and he'd dutifully pick me up. For years I was, essentially, of no fixed address. My dad let me work my way through this.

In the end, I never moved out. I waited around until Mom just stopped providing a home. It took four years. I had just turned sixteen.

~~~~~~

On a cold winter morning, Mom entered the food bank for the first time in her life. She had not had a meal in two days. She and Stephen had bought a box of wine with their last few dollars. It would be another three days before Stephen received his modest paycheque from the pizza joint he cooked at. Mom called me from a pay phone to see if I could pick her up. The two brown paper bags were too heavy for her to carry. I made my way down in my newly acquired 1983 Honda Civic.

The food bank was on Medicine Hat's busiest road, Kingsway Avenue. It straddled the railroad tracks. When I arrived I took the bags from Mom's arms and piled them into the trunk, slamming the lid and getting back into the car as fast as I could. I hoped that nobody would see me.

We drove down the laneway and stopped at the corner. As I tried to find an opening in traffic to get back onto Kingsway, I glanced over and Mom lowered her head.

"We're moving," she said.

"Where?"

She nodded towards the tracks.

I looked up, letting my eyes focus in the distance. I knew exactly where she was moving. I saw the big old dilapidated brick building right across the street from the railway. The sign hung by a wire above the once-grand entryway of Medicine Hat's first posh hotel. My mom was moving into the Cecil.

I looked at her with tears in my eyes.

"Oh, Mom."

We wept quietly all the way home.

Like the ships off the Magdalen Islands coast, my mom's life was shipwrecked.

Dad was worried about what the wreckage would do to me. Soon after Mom's move, he asked me to go for a drive with him. We hadn't gone for a no-reason drive since I was six. We drove around town for an hour or so, then up to the world's largest tee-pee. Town Council had brought it to Medicine Hat after Calgary showcased it during the 1988 Winter Olympics. We got out and circled around it. The wind was howling and blowing through the painted poles. Dad seemed uncertain. We got back in the Suburban.

"Let's try something. Together," Dad said.

A few minutes later, Dad parked at the Provincial Building on 3rd Street. We walked through the lobby and down the hall. It still smelled of new paint and engineered air. We walked past the Licence Bureau, the By-Law Office, and Family Services. We stopped at a frosted glass door. A sign that looked like it had just been hung read: AL-ANON. I had no idea what it stood for.

The door was locked. Dad knocked and a kind-looking woman answered and welcomed us in.

"We're just getting underway."

I flashed Dad a look: *getting what underway?*

The office had a small front desk and seven black folding chairs set up in a circle. The woman we had spoken to went to sit at the top of the circle. Three younger kids were already seated. Another woman stood with her back against the wall. Dad sat down and I sat beside him.

I sat in shame and hunched my back, feeling relief in not knowing the three kids beside me. I don't remember what we discussed at the meeting. Everything was drowned out by the ringing voice in my head: *I am not a victim.* I hated the pity I saw in the counsellor's gaze. I could feel my cheeks redden.

A few days later, Mom called me from a pay phone asking me to come by and visit. I didn't want to. I didn't want to see her there. I didn't want to be *seen* there. I pleaded to take her for lunch or coffee instead. She refused. I had no choice.

I parked at the side of the building. Inside, the lobby was smoke-stained and dark. It took me a minute to orientate myself when I stepped in from the bright afternoon light. It stank of stale beer, cigarette smoke, and decades of neglect. The stairs to the right took me to the basement. As I descended, I remembered Al-Anon's discussion about the addict's rock bottom. I was descending into Mom's, one dirty step at a time.

I knocked on the apartment door. When it opened, I saw what rock bottom looked like. The apartment was one step away from homelessness. The kitchen had a small table and two rickety wooden chairs, a sink, and a makeshift counter with a Bunsen burner on top for cooking. There was a beer fridge in the corner by the bathroom door. The living room had a couch, a low table that housed the cigarette rolling machine, and a television, the only item of value that had not yet been taken to the pawnshop. The bedroom had a closet, a broken dresser, and a queen-size mattress lying on the floor. Clothes were strewn about. There were no windows. The air stank of musty smoke, and the smell of stale beer permeated everything.

At rock bottom, you float up or you drown. Mom did not float. The weight of the water above was too heavy. She was drowning.

She did try. She fought. She gulped for air. Most nights erupted into a vodka-fuelled screaming match. She'd throw what was left of their ornamental possessions, a small Inuit carving or a brass vase. It would smash into one of their few unbroken picture frames. He would throw her to the ground. She would lie there crying on the dingy floor. He would go for more vodka in the tavern upstairs.

She'd always call me during the lull in the violence. It would be late. One time, not long after she moved into the Cecil, she called me at Dad's at two in the morning. I knew, even before I picked up the bedroom phone, that she would be drunk. Her speech was slurred, hurried, and desperate, as it always was those days. She was making a break for it. She couldn't take this life, the abuse. She asked me if I could come and get her. This time was different, she said.

I made myself believe it every time. I had made this run before. It always made me nervous. No; scared. In a storm, you just never know what could happen; what the force of the storm could do. I never knew what shape my mom would be in when the door opened. I never knew if Stephen would be there, or if he'd return while I was there.

This time the door was left ajar, so I peeked in. Mom was in the bedroom, in the midst of throwing her tattered Friday Image blouses into a garbage bag. She was crying. The light in the room was burnt out. Only the kitchen light worked. I called out to her. She told me to grab her purse on the couch and make sure some smokes were in it.

I waited with her purse, hoping the door would not open. Mom hurried. When she emerged from the bedroom, she looked like she hadn't slept in a week. Her hair was knotted, her eyes were red with tears, and her face looked cigarette-skin grey.

"Let's go!" she cried.

I grabbed her bag, cracked the door, and peeked down the hallway. There was only one way out of the basement. I waved her through and we were off. I don't think Mom even closed the door behind her. I took her hand as we were about to start up the stairs. Then I heard a voice around the corner. Two drunks. I stopped. We stood motionless at the foot of the stairs. Mom breathed heavily. She hadn't stopped crying.

Once the voices faded, we climbed the stairs, made a break for the front door, and fast-walked to my car. I threw the garbage bag in the back seat as Mom settled into the passenger side. Her eyes darted across the street, down the alley, to the reflection in the rear-view mirror.

I peeled out of the Cecil's gravel parking lot. It was 2:30 a.m. I had no idea where I was going from there. It didn't really matter; anyplace was better. We drove back up to Crescent Heights. She was glad to be out of the hotel; I wanted to be closer to our past. But there are no motels in Crescent Heights and it was too late to drive to Calgary. I took her to the Sun-Deck hotel on the outskirts of town, by the airport. It was a typical two-storey cinderblock motel, a way station for truck drivers and frugal motorists. Mom was coming off of her drunk a little. She sat at the edge of one double bed with her head in her hands. I threw the garbage bag on the other bed and tried to comfort her.

We ordered a pepperoni and mushroom pizza from Farroh's. She ate. She was still shaking like a leaf. I put a blanket over her and she fell asleep. I crawled into the other bed and did the same.

The next morning, we woke up at the same time. She was sober. Her only hangover was fear. I went out and got two breakfast sandwiches, two coffees, and two orange juices at the A&W across the highway. When I got back, Mom was in the shower. She came out looking better. A little more like herself. She ate again.

We tried to put a game plan together. I pleaded with her to let me take her to Calgary. She could stay with Grandpa Ralph, dry out, maybe get a job. She was unsure. She was, more than anything, an addict. She needed alcohol, even if it came with the life she was living. I managed to convince her to stay another night so we could talk more about it. She knew I had to go to work that afternoon; she was buying time. When I came back after my shift, I went to the motel office to pay for another night.

"Two-oh-three? Another night?" The lady looked at me, confused.

Mom had checked out.

There were many more late-night rescue attempts. Once we even made it onto Highway One en route to Calgary. But Mom sobered up by Gleichen and made me turn back.

A year later, the only trips we were making together were to the women's shelter. During a violent fight, the bartenders upstairs would hear the noise and someone would call the police. I'd drive down to the Cecil hoping that the cops had beat me there. I was so preoccupied with each particular emergency, on each particular night, that I never saw the headlights of my dad's Chevy Suburban following me. I never knew.

The Cecil Hotel is close to the police station, so the cops were often there before I arrived. Sometimes they'd take Stephen to jail for the night. Sometimes they'd take them both. But usually I'd take Mom to the shelter. There, the fear dripped from the walls; it pooled on the floor. I could not stay very long. The staff were cautious and secretive in order to protect the women and children under their care. Fear filled everyone's eyes, the same fear I had seen so many years ago in the eyes of the animals Mom was saving at the S.P.C.A. Whenever Mom was at the shelter, she would act as if she were a volunteer taking care of the other women in the house, looking after their children, helping the staff. She was not in their care, she was assisting with the care. This was not happening to her.

The ghosts of brutality haunted that women's shelter. The men who place their wives and children in such a situation have an appetite that feeds off others' fear. It is cowardice of the worst kind. My car would be filled with murderous *mens rea* every time I left. I hated what going there did to me, the slow burn of rage that it lit, the certainty that she'd return. The inability to make the cycle stop.

How could my mom be here? How had it come to this? How could I put an end to it? But I knew, in truth, that my mom was stuck at rock bottom. She had one escape—alcohol. And it pushed her deeper.

In my heart, I knew there just wasn't anything more she could give. My mom—the mom I had known as a child, that vibrant, healthy, loving, firecracker of a woman—had been extinguished. She was gone. She was not coming back.

Mom always returned to the Cecil's basement. She found crevices in the rock's bottom into which to sink deeper. Soon she was rarely leaving the apartment. Once the apartment became her universe, she rarely left her windowless bedroom. She would lie for days in the dark on a mattress on the floor. Stephen would bring her food and wine. Sometimes she ate; she always drank.

I knew she was lost to me. I knew there wasn't a thing I could do about it. And that made me mad. It forced me to question the power of love.

Then, just when I needed it, someone came into my life who answered that question.

~~~~~

Jade. I adored her from the moment I saw her.

She had just moved to Medicine Hat from Assiniboia, Saskatchewan. The first time I saw her—actually only half of her—I fell for her fully. Our school lockers were in the same hallway. I remember catching a glimpse of part of her face behind her locker door before she clicked her lock closed and headed for the end of the hallway. I was smitten.

She, not so much. She thought I was arrogant and loud-mouthed. She was more right than wrong. In any event, I had my work cut out for me. It took me four years and a ballet to make my case.

My dad was promoting the Alberta Ballet's tour stop in Medicine Hat. The company was performing *Swan Lake*. Tickets for the college theatre sold out quickly. Jade had been dancing since she was four years old and she was desperate to go. So Jade's mom called my dad to see if there were any spare tickets. There were not, but Dad offered Jade a gig ushering for the night. She could sit on the stairs and watch the show if she wanted. Susan told me this. She knew under the circumstances I'd quickly become interested in the fate of Odette and Siegfried.

After folks were seated, the lights went down and the curtain came up. I scooched beside Jade on the fifth stair at stage right. I couldn't see a thing on stage. I couldn't have cared less. Watching Jade watch the dancers was life-changing for me. An artist watching art. Including the "May I sit here?" that I had just spoken, I had probably said fewer than a hundred words to her. But I remember sitting on that fifth stair and thinking: *This is the girl for me.* Sixteen years later, when the marriage videographer asked one of my groomsmen, Ryan Hehr, if I had told him when I knew I was going to propose to Jade, he laughed and said it was the night before our first date.

At summer's end, Jade and I moved to Calgary. Jade taught ballet at a small dance studio. She rented a suite from a friend. Eric Van Enk, a lanky, toothy Dutch friend, and I rented an apartment just a few blocks west, close to the university. It was an arrangement that worked out well. Eric was dating Jade's roommate, so we would alternate places.

Whatever my student loan didn't cover, working with my uncle Ron made up for. Though he was the most successful music promoter in the country, he still behaved like the eldest brother, making sure everyone in the family was okay. He'd have me work all the concerts he brought into Calgary. Halfway through a show, he'd pull me aside and slip a handful of bills into my jacket pocket. The money would pay my rent and allow me to take Jade out for dinner.

Jade and I were together all the time. We were together when I received my law school application response from Dalhousie. I held the sealed letter in my hand and called her. We met in the living room of her suite. She sat down on the couch, her feet together and her hands folded, her back straight. She wanted a no. I wanted a yes. I opened the letter. I had my way.

We both smiled. We had some decisions to make. We had a quiet dinner at her house and went to bed. I did, anyway. Jade sat up the entire night, thinking about moving to Halifax, a city we knew nothing about, thousands of miles away. That night, she tried to decide whether she was going to marry me or not. It took her all night. I think I just squeaked by. The next morning, her eyes were red with tiredness. But she was smiling.

"Let's go," she said.

We made a list of things to do once we got to Halifax.

1. Find a place to live.
2. Make friends.

That was as far as we got. We spent the rest of the day in bed.

We went back to Medicine Hat to say goodbye to our families and pick up a few items that we had left behind. At Jade's parents' place, we packed the last few inches of empty space into our weighed down Volkswagen Jetta. Dad was there to see us off. He said he was proud of me and to drive safely. Then he reached into his fanny pack and handed me thirty fifty-dollar bills.

"Gas money," he said.

When we pulled out of the driveway, I saw Jade's mom collapse into my dad's arms. She was inconsolable. Jade didn't stop crying until we reached the outskirts of Regina.

As Jade slept and I drove, I wondered why I was so insistent on moving to Halifax. Why put everyone through all this? There were plenty of good schools close to home. I didn't know the answer, but I knew I felt lighter with each glance in the rear-view mirror.

We fell in love with our new city. Everything there was new. Except for the lingering concern about my mom. Two thousand miles couldn't deter that uninvited guest. But we would be returning before we knew it.

The mid-December air was thick with fog. Our taxi driver struggled to wind through downtown Halifax. He thought we were crazy to go to the airport. He knew we'd be socked in. He was right. We sat at the airport waiting for the sun to rise and burn the fog off. It took five hours.

When we landed in Medicine Hat, the sky was crystal blue. We dropped our bags off at Jade's parents' and I popped down to Grandma's for a visit. As I opened the door, the sweet smell of rice vinegar filled my nostrils. Grandma was busy making *inari* sushi. She wiped her hands, hugged me, and put on the kettle. We sat and had cups of *ocha*. We talked about my first semester of law school, how we were getting along in Halifax, the weather, who was coming down from Lethbridge over the holidays, the carpal tunnel in her left forearm, how busy Dad had been, and how quiet Grandpa Sak had been. The usual.

Then she suddenly shot up and looked around left to right. "I have some money. This is hush-hush."

When it came to money with Grandma, it was always "hush-hush." She pulled a crisp, new one-hundred-dollar bill from her pocket and handed it to me. I protested. My student loan was coming in the next two weeks, I was fine. But I knew it was futile to resist. I thanked her and took the money.

My heart sank a little as I left Grandma's because my next stop was to see Mom. It was always a crapshoot. I just didn't know what I was walking into. And I had no way of knowing; her phone had been disconnected again. I parked in the side lot of the Cecil and girded myself with each step. I took a deep breath as I opened the hotel lobby door. The stairwell down to the basement seemed darker and dingier than the last time I had descended it. I stood at her apartment door listening for any clues as to what was happening on the other side. Silence.

I knocked and heard a faint hello from my mom.

"It's me, Mom."

"Mark!" Her voice sounded excited, but it took her an awfully long time to walk the ten steps from the living room couch—I was sure that's where she'd been—to the apartment door.

When she opened it, I tried to hide my shock, my shame, my disappointment and disdain. But my eyes betrayed me. I knew she saw all of it.

She looked like a skeleton. Her bones poked out of her pale papery skin. Her fingers were so nicotine stained they looked burnt. It seemed as if she'd been sitting on the couch drinking and smoking the whole time I had been gone.

We moved over to the couch. Walking was becoming difficult for her. The running shoes she had bought second-hand were just too heavy. But it was all the store had that fit her.

We spoke about my studies, my new school, my new city. She was trying to keep the conversation about me. When she got up to go to the washroom, I snuck over to the small beer fridge in the kitchen. I opened the door as quietly as I could, hoping she would not hear. There was a bottle of black bean sauce, a box of cheap white wine, a bottle of mustard, and two end pieces from a loaf of bread. I lost myself in the bleakness of that fridge. Mom startled me when she opened the bathroom door. She hadn't flushed the toilet.

"Oh, Stephen is bringing pizza home when he's done his shift," she assured me when she saw what I was looking at. I nodded.

She limped over to me. "It's so nice to see you."

"You too, Mom."

I suggested we go out and get her some new shoes. She demurred. After a few minutes of probing, I got her to confess she hadn't left the apartment in over a month. Going out brought on crippling panic attacks. She said she had agoraphobia. It kept her prisoner. She hadn't seen or felt the sun in more than forty days. She hadn't breathed fresh air. I looked around the apartment—it was a tomb.

It took an hour of persistence, but I convinced her to go out with me. As we left, I had to help her up the stairs. She was shaky on her feet and her hands were trembling; she was concentrating on containing her fear.

I only had the one hundred dollars that Grandma had just given me, but I wanted to get Mom some new shoes. Walmart had just opened in Medicine Hat, so we went there. Mom smiled at the Walmart greeter like we were walking into a luxury hotel.

"This is my son. He's home from law school." I smiled and held her arm.

We walked through an aisle stacked with women's shoes. We found a few size six runners. I helped Mom sit down on a padded stool at the end of the aisle. The first pair were far too wide. Mom's feet were slivers of flesh. The second seemed better. I laced her up, hunching over like Dad used to do when he tied my skates. The shoes felt light and they fit. I looked up to see what she thought. She was in tears. She hadn't had a new pair of shoes in over a decade.

"They fit perfectly," she said quietly.

Mom was walking a little better as we left. We returned to her apartment.

That was one of the last times I would see her. Standing in her decrepit kitchen, holding on to the counter to stand tall in her new, bright white sneakers.

I told her I loved her and I closed the door.
How could I?
How could I have closed that door?

CHAPTER 14

The Boys Are on Their Way

In the winter of 2001, I was preparing for my final exams in second-year law. I would study in the bedroom while Jade was in the living room.

The phone rang and I picked it up.

"Mark."

I almost dropped the receiver. I'd never spoken to Stephen on the phone. His voice was shaky, broken.

"Your mom is sick."

No shit.

"Where are you?" I asked, already knowing the answer. I could hear the hospital's intercom paging someone in the background.

"She's *really* sick."

"Is there a doctor or a nurse there?"

He put the receiver aside. I was glad for that. I could hear him ask the nurse to speak with me. "He's in Halifax. He's a lawyer," he said.

I was glad I was in the bedroom. I knew I was going to need a moment alone after the call. I could hear the surprise in the nurse's voice. "Are you Diane's son?"

"I am."

"Well, she is very sick. If I were you, I would come home as soon as you can."

I'm ashamed to admit that the first thing to cross my mind was that I'd miss all my exams.

"Okay," was all I could manage. "Can I speak to her?"

"She is not able to speak at this point."

Fuck. Fuck. Fuck. My stomach tied itself into a knot. I started to ask the same question with different words: How bad was she? What was the problem? But the only real question was: could she survive? I couldn't ask that one.

The nurse didn't have it in her to tell me. She put me on hold to talk to the attending doctor. She spoke across the ICU desk. "It's Diane's son. He's calling from Halifax. He's a lawyer."

The nurse was being kind. She was humanizing Mom. The doctor clearly saw a yellowed skeletal vagabond in the bed down the hall. My being in law school made her more real, worthy of his time. But being in law school did not make me a better son. She was still dying in the bed down the hall. The doctor picked up the phone.

"Hi, I was just with your mom. She is very sick. You should come home right away if you can."

"Is she going to die?"

"Yes."

I had known this was coming. But I began to panic all the same.

"Is there anything that can be done? Surgery?"

"Mark—it's Mark, right? Your mom is well past that. I'd come home on the next flight."

Mom was *well past that*. It's impossible to say when she had exceeded the point of no return. But I know one thing: when she did, she did it by herself. She was all alone. Her eldest son was busy living his life on the other side of the country.

I was still shell-shocked on the plane the next morning. How could this happen? How could I be two thousand miles away from this?

Somewhere over New Brunswick, the thought hit me like a tsunami.

If I could abandon my own mother, who in my life was safe?

It's a fear I thought I'd never fully shake.

Daniel greeted me at the Calgary airport. He had been early; he had been waiting. We hugged but said nothing.

It was a bitterly cold night as we drove the Number One south to Medicine Hat. The windows were iced over. We didn't speak much during that two-and-a-half hour drive. It was dark when we passed the Gas City sign.

We drove straight to the hospital. Daniel knew the room number. We took the elevator up to the sixth floor. Mom was lying on her back, asleep, alone in the dark room. The purple blouse and pants that she and Donna Stetic had picked out from Friday's Image were neatly folded on the chair in the far corner.

There were two red roses in a thin glass vase on the bedside table. Our dad had been there already. He had said his goodbyes. I saw his handwriting on the little square card.

The boys are on their way.

She had been bathed. Her hair was soft. It was whiter than I had ever seen it. Her hands were clean, even under her fingernails. Her fingers retained only a faint shade of yellow. She looked so very peaceful. Her thin arms were outside the bedding, which was perfectly folded right under them. I'd never seen her sleep like that. She always slept on her side, usually out of the blankets with the bottom folded up over her legs. But she was not really sleeping now. She was essentially in a coma. Her teeth were grinding a little, but she did not speak.

We both whispered into her ear. *We love you. We are here.*

Daniel and I lingered in the hospital room for two hours before leaving for the night. At home, we hugged Dad and Susan at the door. They had been sitting on the floor in the entryway, waiting for us. They would have been sitting there had we come home at 3 a.m. We had tea. We cried. We waited.

The next morning, the rest of the MacLean family arrived—Grandpa Ralph, Uncle Doug, Uncle Blake and Aunt Marilyn.

We grasped at straws. We asked about organ transplants. But it wasn't just her liver. Her kidneys seemed to be failing. She was only fifty-one but everything was shutting down. Her body was broken. We knew that. Her spirit had been broken for many years. Without that larger-than-life spirit, her small frame withered.

She was lost.

We met at the hospital to say our final goodbyes. Grandpa and I went down to the Tim Hortons in the lobby. We talked about funeral details. We were avoiding seeing her in that state. Avoiding having to face the grim reality of the situation.

Stephen came by early in the afternoon. He had taken something to calm his nerves. He was clearly in a lot of pain. He was shaking and said very little. When he did speak, it was lighter than a whisper. Grandpa—the old soldier—was upset. His little girl was dying and he was beside himself. We all were, except for Daniel. He kept his head. He was still my fearless little brother.

Twenty minutes into our tea, Daniel came rushing out of the elevator.

"You have to come now. Mom's up."

We moved as quickly as we could. The elevator seemed to take an eternity. As we rode it up, Daniel said, "She sat up. Her eyes were open. The nurse said some people do that just before . . ." His voice trailed off.

When the elevator doors opened, we speed-walked down the hall. As we turned the corner into the room, I heard the nurse say, "She's going."

Everyone was crying. Uncle Doug stood a few feet away and was looking up at the ceiling. He was whispering, *You're loved, you're loved, you're loved.*

Daniel and I took our places at her side. We leaned in close. I stroked her head. We kissed her face. One last time, between her Bookends, she closed her eyes and shifted a little.

I felt her final breath on my left cheek.

Good night, Mom. Love you.

I hoped she felt as if it were 1986. I hoped she remembered Daniel's ruddy, round face smiling at her. I hoped she saw me looking at her, biting one side of my lip. I hoped she was caressing my face, telling me I had a golden heart.

The morning after my mom's death was the coldest day of the year in Medicine Hat. The back deck railing was caked in ice. It looked like it had just rolled in off the North Atlantic.

It was how I felt. Ice cold.

Mom hadn't wanted a funeral. She never did anything for show. Why should she have one now?

But funerals are for the living. We needed closure, we needed one another. We gathered a few days later at the Saamis Memorial Funeral Chapel, a converted old brick farmhouse at the bottom of Scholten Hill, at the opposite end of Kingsway from the food bank.

Mom hadn't known a preacher. So we brought in a sergeant from the Salvation Army. At 11 a.m., people began to arrive. Daniel and I greeted everyone at the door—cousins, friends from City Hall . . . the faces washed over me. Daniel and I waited until everyone was in and then took our places in the first pew to the left. In a court of law, it's where the defendant would have sat. Bagpipes played. The minister said a few words. I heard hardly any of it.

Then it was our turn to speak. Daniel and I walked up the three steps. Daniel read a letter first. I can't remember a single word he said. When he finished he stepped to the side, and I put my hands on each side of the lectern. I was bracing myself. Daniel softly placed his hand on mine. Immediately I pulled my hand away. I was afraid if I felt any softness, I'd crumble.

I asked the folks in the room to remember my mom as she once was, to remember her spirit, her grace, her spunk. I told them to remember their delight, not their sorrow, to let those memories—those delights—be her final resting place. I told friends and family I had found solace. I lied: I felt neither grace nor solace. I felt fear. I felt a mighty undercurrent and I was petrified it would sweep me under.

I felt ashamed. I felt guilty.

After Christmas, I packed up for my return to Halifax. I had just one stop to make before heading out of town. I had to pick up Mom's ashes.

I drove back to the funeral home. What was left of her cremated body was handed to me packed into a white plastic medicine bottle. Her name was taped to it. She was bottle number S7. I packed her into my suitcase, wrapped in a plastic Safeway grocery bag.

I thought I was fine.

I was wrong.

I began drifting before the jet's wheels touched down in Halifax. I did not sleep for three days. Jade was relieved to have me home and under her careful, watchful eyes. I pretended to be happy to see her. The blues and whites of late-night television washed over my dull face. I knew she was lying in bed, eyes wide open too. I knew she knew.

I maintained my routine. Shower, breakfast, class. I mastered the art of pretense. Everything was good. Except I did not take a single note in class for six weeks. I did not touch Jade in as many weeks. Night after night, I'd fall asleep in front of the television. I'd wake and stare blankly at the set for another few hours, waiting for dawn. I'd be out of the apartment before Jade awoke. The lectures washed over me. Constitutional Law, Evidence, Taxation. I couldn't have cared less. I'd go for late-night walks in Point Pleasant Park. I'd stand at the water's edge. The high midnight moon would use the ocean as a dance floor. Its clarity would pierce me.

I was dulling myself. I was terrified. I could not shake the fear that had overcome me in the plane somewhere over New Brunswick. That fear struck me at my core. It was paralyzing.

I was sleeping a couple hours a night. Around midnight, Jade would come out of the bathroom after washing up. She would lean over me on the couch and ask me to come to bed. I wouldn't even look up.

"In a bit."

She'd touch my shoulder or my arm as she left the room. I'd fall back asleep on the couch. Some nights, I'd wake and drag myself to bed. Most nights, I wouldn't.

This went on for three months. We spoke little. She was waiting for me to turn a corner that I could not even see. She was patient. I was lost. One night around 4 a.m., I came to bed. The moon was full. Jade was sitting up, looking out the window. I could see she hadn't slept all night. I sat on the side of the bed. She slowly turned to face me.

"Do you still love me?" she asked. She had been asking herself this question all night long. Tears pooled in her harvest-moon eyes.

I felt my spine slump. I knew at that moment I had hit my own rock bottom.

"Jade, I'm sorry. I'm in this fog. The only thing I know for sure is the answer to that question."

She had been my horizon. Behind me, in front of me, I had seen only her. But in that moment she seemed so far away. I seemed so far away from myself. We held each other as we fell asleep in our tiny, moonlit bedroom.

"Remember what you're made of," she said.

I cried tears of gratitude. For her. For Grandma Mitsue and Grandpa Ralph—for showing me a way out.

After that night, things gradually improved for me. I bounced back. Jade pulled me up, pulled me out. Life regained colour. My studies became interesting again. I volunteered on a few political campaigns. Mostly, I stuck close to Jade.

The night before I graduated from law school, I rented the Queen's Suite at the Westin Nova Scotian. We could see our apartment from the massive balcony. That night, it felt as if we had never left the stairs of the college theatre. I proposed to my best friend. Jade told me that, in her mind, she had said yes three years earlier.

I was offered a job at a Bay Street law firm, and we moved to Toronto a week later. One day that summer, my friend Sachin Aggarwal, a political organizer, asked me to join him on the patio at the Café Diplomatico in Little Italy. We had hardly said hello when he asked me what I thought of Michael Ignatieff. I had read most of his books while studying political science. I had especially liked *Blood and Belonging*. We discussed pros and cons as if the author weren't a real person. Ignatieff was smart, good. His stand on the Iraq War, bad. All in all, a very interesting person with real potential to make an impact. The conversation did not have a speculative air to it.

"He's willing to run?" I said doubtfully.

"We're going to see tomorrow. Why don't you join the conversation?"

I was curious, so I went. A small group of Liberals, some middle-aged, some young, met Michael in one of the towers in which I had recently interviewed. He was indeed keen to run for the party. He wanted to discuss details. Which riding? How much money would we need to raise? How would the prime minister react? Mostly he wanted to know two things of the strangers seated around the table. Could we deliver? Could we be trusted? Michael was more concerned with the first question. His wife, Zsuzsanna Zsohar, a fierce Hungarian, was determined to know the answer to the second question.

After Michael and Zsuzsanna left, we charted out a small tour for Michael. He hadn't lived in Canada for some time; there were many people to meet and many places to visit. We all lived in Toronto, so that was easy. So was Ottawa and Montreal.

Who knows anyone in Calgary? I put up my hand.

Who knows anyone in Halifax? I put up my hand.

"Okay, that settles it. Sakamoto will run the first tour."

Political tours aren't much different than concert tours. Having worked with my uncle Ron on his music business, coordinating this tour was like hopping on a bike after years without riding. It is, after all, show biz. As we travelled together, Michael would become professorial, expounding on Cartier's first exploratory voyage of 1534 as we flew across the Gulf of St. Lawrence, or walking me through Riel and the North-West Rebellion of 1885 as we passed high above the prairies. I was always more concerned about getting him and Zsuzsanna to our destination on time and in one piece.

Our first tour ended in Calgary. We spent the day meeting local folks, oil executives, and a few journalists. Then I escorted them back to their hotel room.

"Okay, guys," I said, "I'm off to visit my brother. I'll be back at 7 a.m. tomorrow to get you to the airport."

Michael stopped me on the way out and told me that he wanted me to know he and Zsuzsanna were both fond of me. I smiled and bowed my head a little. I had become fond of them too.

I remained close to them throughout the coming months and years. When Michael became Leader of the Opposition, he asked me to come to Ottawa and work with him. Jade was reluctant. She didn't want to live in Ottawa, but she didn't want me to work out of town either. I told Michael that I could help out for only six months.

During those six months, shuttling between my home in Toronto and Parliament Hill, I almost felt like I lived at Toronto's island airport. During the week, I shared a condo with two old political pals, Alexis Levine and Sachin Aggarwal. My bedroom consisted of two mattresses, a toiletries bag, and the clothes I had brought with me that week.

My first day at the office was a cold, dreary one. The hairs on the back of my neck stood on end as I made my way up to Parliament Hill for the first time as an active participant. I stopped for a moment at the centennial flame. It flickered and danced. I thought of all the nights Mom and I had tuned in to watch Knowlton Nash. I was a long way from my Superman pyjamas and peanut butter toast. I was a long way from Medicine Hat. I was a long way from my mom. I tried to push that thought out of my mind. I did not want to be late for my first meeting.

The Leader's of the Opposition's office is a cavernous, wood-panelled room. A few people huddled around Michael's table. A hundred decisions awaited: staff hires, parliamentary positions, scheduling, Question Period, short-term strategy. We spoke for thirty minutes, then broke to get the first news cycle of the day and some breakfast.

As we walked out of his office, Michael pointed to the large room next door, the Opposition boardroom. "That was King's War Room," he said. The current Opposition boardroom was never meant to be the Prime Minister's Office. But Mackenzie King loved that room. When he was elected prime minister in 1920, he refused to relinquish it. In politics, real estate is everything. For the duration of King's reign, that room remained the Prime Minister's Office. He personally saw to its total renovation. HONOUR THY KING was inscribed in the archway above the boardroom's main entry. Every major Canadian decision about the Second World War took place between those four walls.

I took a deep breath. I had a meeting in that room in thirty minutes.

I tried to maintain my composure while I met a few Members of Parliament in King's War Room. The meeting lasted about thirty minutes and I don't recall a single word spoken. I was thinking about the men who had once met around that very table, reviewing reports, sipping water, writing notes. Making decisions.

Like the decision to send Ralph Augustus MacLean to war.

Like the decision to intern Mitsue and Hideo Sakamoto.

The decisions made within this room had sealed my grandparents' fate. They had been condemned there, apprehended there, abandoned there. They had been left for dead there.

That room had taken my grandpa MacLean to the brink of death. It had tried, convicted, and sentenced my Japanese grandparents. Perhaps, just perhaps, Prime Minister King had sat right where I was sitting now as he decided to intern every Canadian of Japanese descent, and when the decision was made to send two thousand young men to serve as a tripwire for fifty thousand battle-hardened Japanese soldiers.

The decisions made right where I was sitting had caused tears, blood, and unspeakable hardship. I hated that room for what it had done to those I loved. And yet, but for the decisions made in that room, I most certainly would not be sitting there at all. I would not exist. But for the internment, my grandparents would never have left British Columbia for the cold, hard, southern Alberta prairies. But for his imprisonment, Grandpa MacLean would never have met my grandma when the returning soldiers stopped in Calgary to receive a hero's welcome.

Life happens one decision at a time. You have no idea where each will take you. Maybe it is fate. Maybe it is God's will. Maybe everything does happen for a reason. All I know is that you have to find a reason in it. The reason is usually the future. I was inching closer to forgiveness.

As I sat in King's War Room, the sun broke through thick clouds, its light filtering in through the massive arched windows. The brightness seemed to open the room to me. And then it opened my country to me, illuminating, in that moment, in how precious few places in the world my family's story—my grandparents', my parents', and mine—would be possible.

Someone's assistant knocked on the door. The room was booked for another meeting shortly. He must have wondered why I looked like I had just seen the face of God.

CHAPTER 15

Journey's End

Six months in Ottawa turned into a year. On a Tuesday morning, Jade called. She usually didn't call quite as early as she did that day. She was nervous, I could tell. She couldn't hold in her news for the forty-eight hours it would take for me to get back to Toronto.

"I'm pregnant."

I beamed. Just beamed.

"I'm coming home."

Nine months later, almost to the day, I sat alone in the hallway at St. Joseph's Health Centre. Jade was on the other side of the green door. The baby was breach, so we had opted for a C-section. I watched as the doctors scrubbed up in an adjacent room. They were talking about their summer vacations. One to Italy, the other to France. After they entered the operating room through the side door, a nurse came to escort me in. I stood up, made sure my shoes were still covered by the hospital booties, shifted my gown, and straightened out my hairnet.

The operating room was crowded with medical equipment, two doctors, and three nurses. I walked around the curtain that shielded

Jade's abdomen to see her face. She was trying to be strong, but she was scared. There were tears in her eyes.

The doctor popped his head around the curtain.

"We are about to start. We'll be done in about five minutes."

Jade nodded and grasped my hand. I stroked her forehead. Her body shook a little as the doctors tugged at her on the other side of the curtain.

In a few minutes, a nurse declared: "It's a girl! Ten fingers, ten toes!"

I kissed Jade's cheek and she clutched my hand a little tighter. The nurse came around the curtain and put our little baby girl on the side gurney. She cleaned her off, prepping her for her first breath. I could see the baby move on the table, reacting to the touch of the towel. And then that newborn wail rang out.

We both took a deep breath as our hearts soared. The nurse brought the baby close, a few pictures were taken, and then, suddenly, everyone was gone. Jade was rolled out to the recovery room. The last nurse in the room handed me the baby.

"Here you go, Dad," she said, and then she left.

It was just the two of us. The room seemed much larger with the instruments cleared away. I looked down at our baby. I took two steps towards the door. She shifted. I stopped. She stilled herself. I had one foot in the room and one foot in the hallway when she opened her eyes wide. She was staring right at me. Doctors will say a baby cannot see so soon after arriving in the world. But I know she saw me. It took one look, just one, to vanquish the fear that had struck me in the plane high over New Brunswick.

I stayed the night in the hospital. While Jade was recovering I paced the room with the baby. Fear gone, I knew I had a job to do. I had to come to this task with an open heart. I could feel the sadness rising. I wished Mom would open the door and peek in, hold the baby. Laugh, cry, smile. I knew I had to make my peace with her. So I could laugh, cry, and smile. Jade woke and grimaced as she sat up. She held out her arms and I placed the little one in her arms. They were beautiful together.

The night before we went into the hospital, I had been reading *The Tale of Genji* aloud. I had told Jade I liked the name Miya.

Jade looked at me now. It was dawn.

"How about Miya Mitsue?"

I nodded and choked out a thank you.

My grandparents bore witness to the worst in humanity. Yet they also managed to illuminate the finest in humanity. Their hearts were my home. I saw none of the ugliness they had. I felt none of the bitterness.

How on earth did they manage that?

Forgiveness is moving on. It is a daily act that looks forward. Forgiveness smiles.

I had never said I'm sorry to my mom. She had never sought my forgiveness. Now that she was gone, where could I go from here? Where could I seek salvation? How could I find reprieve from my anger at her for leaving me behind? Could I absolve myself for my own sins? I thought I had missed my opportunity for forgiveness. But I realized now that forgiveness is not a transaction. It is not an exchange. Forgiveness has nothing to do with the past.

Like her love, Mom's forgiveness was a tough forgiveness. It was years in the making. It had peaks and valleys. But Miya Mitsue had brought me to the journey's end. My heart was her home. She deserved room to grow, to be free, to smile.

My mom's final gift to me was forgiveness. It was the hardest lesson she ever taught me.

I was finally ready to let her go.

Saying goodbye, really saying goodbye, is the hardest thing we humans do. We make stuff up—absurd tales—to avoid its searing pain. I had avoided, stalled, hidden, overcompensated, lied, cheated, and closed myself off to avoid that pain. There was just so much unfinished business.

Mom's ashes were still in the white bottle, wrapped in the

plastic Safeway bag, stuffed into a metal business case, and crammed in the back of our bedroom closet.

I flew home to Medicine Hat and rented a car at the Calgary airport. It was dusk and I drove south with the sun setting in my rearview mirror. I listened to Dire Straights's *Brothers in Arms* sixteen times through. I could see Mom smiling and dancing in the living room mirror, green jumpsuit, frosted hair. For those two-and-half hours, in my mind, we were having a ball.

I hadn't given Dad and Susan much of a heads-up about coming home. They knew I was in Alberta, but did not know the purpose of the trip. I didn't want much fanfare. I didn't want a big dinner. I didn't want to deal with other visitors. I just wanted to quietly say goodbye. I wanted to be on my own. I would have stayed at a hotel and been in and out, but you just can't do that in Medicine Hat. You can't get a litre of milk without running into someone you know.

I wanted to be with my mom and I knew where she wanted to be.

I woke up the next morning at Dad's and looked out the back bedroom window. A bright, crisp blue sky was overhead, just the kind of morning Mom loved. I opened the door to the outside and took a deep breath of fresh spring air. I could hear the creek gushing in the valley. I smelled fresh prairie grass. The lone donkey in the pasture was braying loudly. I looked down at my open suitcase. I could see the red S of the Safeway bag.

I had waited a long time for this day. There were times when I thought it might never come to pass. I hopped in the shower, shaved, and clipped my nails. I guess I was getting ready to see her. The smell of coffee hit me halfway up the stairs. Susan was awake, sitting at the kitchen table where she always drank her morning coffee. She was watching a train out the window heading east. Two eggs had already been whipped and last night's vegetables were waiting to be made into an omelette. I sat, had some coffee, and enjoyed breakfast. Normally Dad wouldn't be awake for another few hours, but my surprise visit had thrown him a little. He joined us in his morning *yukata* and juiced a dozen carrots. I downed a glass of it at his insistence.

"I'm going for a drive. I'll be back in a bit," I said.

Susan wanted to know more, I could tell. Dad flashed me a knowing smile. He was piecing it together. He knows some things take time. He does, after all, think in decades.

Back in the bedroom, I threw on a pair of jeans, a sweater, a pair of wool socks, and a down vest. The vest was a little tight over the sweater, which made the plastic pill container feel snug against my body. She felt close. I went back upstairs and put on some sneakers and hurried out the door.

As I drove down Ross Glen Drive, I forgot how to get to Central Park. I had to think of my final destination and work backwards from there. I ended up driving past the Medicine Hat College, down the valley onto Kipling Drive, and then up on Third Avenue. It is no coincidence that Kipling takes you onto Third Avenue, the highest street in Medicine Hat. It shoots straight up. Kipling would have approved mightily. As I crested the hill, I was not sure which way to go. I veered left and was about to take a right turn when I saw the concrete whale. I pulled over at the playground that sits in the southeast corner of the park and got out of the car.

At 10 a.m. on a Tuesday morning, the park was empty. We had it all to ourselves. I put my hand on the concrete whale. It hadn't been painted since I touched it last. I walked the perimeter of the park. It's about two city blocks, lined with tall old poplar trees. The grass was wet with dew. There was no wind. It was just us and two hundred trees.

I looked for the perfect spot. As I walked past the Central Park sign I saw through the ferns an oddly placed bench. There was no path to it, it was all alone. It did not look onto the park. It did not look onto the playground. It sat between two large evergreen trees. When park planners placed the bench there, the trees must have been at a comfortable distance apart. Over the decades they had grown, almost engulfing the bench. Bookends. Perfect.

I sat on the bench and looked up. I wondered if Mom had ever sat here. I wondered how big these two trees would have been back then. Maybe Daniel and I had sat with her in this very spot. The bottle rattled as I opened it. Pieces of her bones were mixed with ashes. The bottle was tightly packed so I was careful not to spill it as I stood up.

I poured Mom in a straight line between the two trees. Her ashes didn't blow into the wind like in the movies, they just fell like sand in an hourglass. I stood beside the bench for a few more minutes, then wrapped the bottle back in the plastic bag and put it into my vest pocket. I smiled and moved on.

Epilogue

Dear Grandma and Grandpa,

Mitsue Margaret Sakamoto and Ralph Augustus MacLean, you are my heroes. You are both heroes in the truest sense of the word. You have borne witness to the worst in humanity—and yet, to so very many you represent humanity's finest.

You are the toughest people I know. You both fought for your country, your dignity, and your lives. Your victory was not that you lived. Your victory was in the way you both went on to live your lives. You refused to be defined by those most injurious of years. You did not dwell there.

You had the strength to move on with hope and optimism. You filled your hearts with faith and forgiveness. You passed that on. Thank God you passed that on.

I have asked much of you. In writing this story, I asked you to take me into the darkest recesses of your memory. The devil, they say, is in the details. I saw him there. But you both walked me through that perilous journey with bravery, with humility, and even—at times—with humour. You showed me your war scars, some plain as day, some hidden.

You faced a fear I hope I will never have to face. For I don't think I'd be as strong. But I do know this: I'm stronger for having your blood course through my veins. You have both—in your own way, and on your own terms—shown me how to lead a loving and honourable life. I hope that as the years unfold I measure up. I promise to try, and in doing so I will feel communion with you for all my days.

So when I say this, it seems just so meagre, but it is all I have to offer:

I thank you.

I thank you and I love you.

Acknowledgments

Forgiveness: A Gift from My Grandparents started out as an essay. Unbeknownst to me, my pal Erin O'Toole wrote to John Stackhouse with a request that he read my family's story. John agreed and promised to publish it as an essay in *The Globe and Mail*—if it was any good. I thank them both for getting the ball rolling. I had no idea where it would take me.

It took me on a journey into history, into my grandparents' memories. It took me on a very personal emotional excavation. It brought me even closer to my grandma Sakamoto and my grandpa MacLean. Over days of marathon interviews and discussions that went well into the night, my understanding of them deepened. I count those nights as some of the most sacred of my life. When the history books and their memories did not seem to align, I sided with their memories. It is, after all, their story.

While publishing a book is a public act, writing is often a solitary one. Yet a chorus of people with generous spirits filled me with encouragement along the way: the entire Hikida family, Darlene Dee, Karning Hum, the staff at the Esplanade Arts & Heritage Centre, Brynne Eaton Auva'a, Kathryn Eaton, Nik Sexton and Kathy Mentier, Jeffrey Remedios, Kevin Bosch, Lanny Bolger,

Janet Eger, Sachin Aggarwal, Abe Schwartz, Joanna Carroll, Joseph Fuda, Lisa Uyeda, Lindsey Love, Ryan Hehr, Shawn Brade, Jord Cowan, Spencer Blair, Eric Van Enk, Samantha McWilliams, Ron and Joyce Sakamoto, Gary and Glory Oseki, Liz McNally, Anthony Gerbrandt, Peter C. Newman, Angie Morris, Gave Lindo, and Myles and Deborah Warken.

Some dear friends were kind enough to speak at length with me as my story took shape: Jon Penney, Naomi Teitel, and Lynndsey Larre. A particular thank you to Michael Ignatieff for his prescient words of advice and encouragement.

I am very thankful for the opportunity HarperCollins Canada offered me in publishing this book. I am grateful to the production team and the promotional team, and to Allyson Latta and Allegra Robinson, whose detailed eye caught more than I'd care to admit. Most of all, I'm indebted to Jim Gifford, my editor. It is a privilege to work with someone who is truly exceptional at what they do. Jim's calming insightfulness pervades this book.

Thanks to my lawyer, agent, and friend, the irreplaceable, indefatigable—likely indestructible—Michael Levine. Without his effort, this book would not have come to be.

I'd give anything for this story to have ended differently. I wish my mom were here with us, here with her grandchildren, Miya, Samuel, and Tomi. Their little souls would have brought so much joy to her life. I am grateful that my dad's loving presence fills my life and theirs. I'm grateful he found Susan. I'm blessed to have my family: Stan and Susan; Daniel, Carly, and Samuel; Cameron and Kim; Chad, Theresa, Emmett, and Calla; Carrick and Amanda; Logan and Kumiko.

I want to offer a special thank you to my brother, Daniel. This is, for better and worse, his story too. I was concerned that publishing parts of our story would impact him negatively. It has not. He urged me to tell our story, our whole story. As a result of this journey I came to admire him even more.

I cannot fathom what I did in some previous life to generate the kind of karma that brought Jade into my life. And if I lived a hundred more lives I couldn't be as proud of the two precious souls our love has brought into this world. Miya and Tomi are all we need. This project essentially left Jade a single parent with two small children. Throughout it all, she shouldered the burden of our family's daily needs and gave me encouragement. More than anything, Jade, I love you.

It is good, finally, to be home.

Photo Captions

p.15. Ralph MacLean (*left*) and Mark Sakamoto en route to the Magdalen Islands, July 14, 2001

p.20. Ralph MacLean (*far right*) and the Uproaders in the Magdalen Islands

p.27. Ford (*left*) and Ralph MacLean outside the family home in the Magdalen Islands

p.52. Mitsue Oseki and Hideo Sakamoto on Hastings Street, Vancouver, July 12, 1941

p.57. Rifleman Ralph MacLean in Gander, Newfoundland, 1940

p.86. Japanese-owned fishing boats confiscated by the Canadian government in the Fraser River in Vancouver

p.100. Mitsue Oseki (*front row, far right*) outside the Japanese-Canadian Centre in Celtic, Vancouver

p.114. Prisoners at North Point POW camp

p.119. Deighton Aitken's grave

p.122. Letter from Ralph MacLean to his mother from North Point POW camp, November 29, 1941

p.131. Collapsed hut at Shamshuipo POW camp, January 1, 1944

p.144. (*From left*) Hanpei, June, Mitsue, and Wari Sakamoto working in the sugar beet fields, Coaldale, Alberta

p.148. Ron (*left*) and Glory Sakamoto in Coaldale, Alberta

p.160. (*From left*) Hanpei, Hideo, and Margaret Sakamoto with Ted Nishimoto in Medicine Hat. Glory and Ron Sakamoto are in the foreground.

p.181. Diane MacLean and Stan Sakamoto in Calgary, Summer 1968

p.183 .(*From left*) Mitsue Sakamoto, Phyllis MacLean, Ralph MacLean, and Stan Sakamoto in Medicine Hat, Spring 1968

p.185. Diane MacLean with Daniel (*left*) and Mark Sakamoto in Medicine Hat, Spring 1983

p.190. Daniel (*left*), and Mark Sakamoto and Ralph MacLean playing chess in Medicine Hat, Summer 1985

"Through stories of starvation and suffering, outright racism and imprisonment, Sakamoto offers a distinct and dark vantage point to Canadian history—one that does away with any geopolitical binaries of good and evil."—*The Globe and Mail*

"Extraordinary and touching."—*Elle Canada*

When the Second World War broke out, Ralph MacLean chose to escape his troubled life on the Magdalen Islands in eastern Canada and volunteer to serve his country overseas. Meanwhile, in Vancouver, Mitsue Sakamoto saw her family and her stable community torn apart after the Japanese attack on Pearl Harbor. Ralph was captured by the Japanese army and would spend the war in prison camps, enduring pestilence, beatings, and starvation. Back in Canada, Mitsue and her family were expelled from their home by the government and forced to spend years eking out an existence in rural Alberta, working other people's land for $1 a day.

By the end of the war, Ralph emerged broken but a survivor. Mitsue, worn down by years of back-breaking labour, had to start all over again in Medicine Hat, Alberta. A generation later, at a high school dance, Ralph's daughter and Mitsue's son fell in love. Although the war had threatened to erase Ralph's and Mitsue's humanity, these two brave individuals somehow surmounted enormous transgressions and learned to forgive. Without this forgiveness, their grandson Mark Sakamoto would never have come to be.

MARK SAKAMOTO, a lawyer by training, has enjoyed a rich and varied career. He began by promoting live music, which led to work with several international acts. He has worked at a Canadian broadcaster and served as a senior political advisor. Both an entrepreneur and an investor in digital health and media, he sits on the board of the Ontario Media Development Corporation. Sakamoto lives in Toronto with his wife and two children. Follow him on Twitter @MarkSakamoto1.

Cover photo courtesy Mark Sakamoto
Author photo by Joseph Fuda

CAN $19.99

HISTORY/MEMOIR ISBN 978-1-44341-798-3

HARPER PERENNIAL
www.harpercollins.ca